The Bedside
Dream
Dictionary

The Bedside Dream Dictionary

500 Dream Symbols and Their Meanings

CANDICE JANCO

FAIR WINDS
PRESS
GLOUCESTER, MASSACHUSETTS

First published in the USA in 2004 by
Fair Winds Press
33 Commercial Street
Gloucester, MA 01930

08 07 06 05 04   1 2 3 4 5

ISBN 1-59233-039-8

Library of Congress Cataloging-in-Publication Data available

Cover design by Laura Shaw
Cover illustration by Elizabeth Cornaro

Printed and bound in Canada

Contents

Introduction

EACH MORNING AS YOU TURN OFF THE ALARM CLOCK and begin your morning routine, the disjointed images of last night's dreams have already begun to disintegrate. Residual images may pop into your mind, but the usual morning mix of low energy and a long to-do list likely causes you to dismiss your dreams with a bemused shrug. You probably don't spend much time interpreting your dreams, because you view them as most people do: psychic scraps left over from a day already too full with commitments, media messages, and visual stimuli. Yet amidst the carpools and office gossip, you may still yearn to connect with your emotions, soul's desires, and life's purpose. The simplest and surest way to gain this level of self-awareness is by listening to and interpreting your dreams. Consider your subconscious your spiritual guide, your psychic gut instinct, and your inner voice.

Dreams are messages from your subconscious self to your conscious self. And like a trusted friend, your subconscious only speaks the truth. *The Bedside Dream Dictionary* was written for those interested in beginning the journey toward self-awareness through dream interpretation. While many dream dictionaries are available for those interested in beginning dream work, they are often based on one particular psychology, such as Freud or Jung, or they are based on witchcraft or precognition. *The Bedside Dream Dictionary* does not adhere to one particular philosophy then adapt each definition to suit that particular pedagogy. Instead, it assumes that the language of your dreams—symbols—have universal meanings based on our collective experiences as human beings.

Just as any language's meaning is determined by the collective experiences of the people who speak it, dream symbols have universal meanings determined by our culture. For example, the symbol "mother" implies nurturing and caring regardless of your native tongue. However, depending upon your experiences with your mother, the symbol may provoke other images as well. Because we all bring to the dream world a different set of experiences, dream symbols can have different meanings for different people. Therefore, every dream is personal even if it contains universal symbols.

The purpose of *The Bedside Dream Dictionary* is to help you understand the universal significance of your dream symbols while acknowledging that each symbol also contains personal truths. Each symbol in the book is followed by a simple and common sense definition, then examples, questions, or actions are provided to help you determine the symbol's personal relevance.

The first step toward understanding the symbols in your dreams is to record your dreams in a dream journal. As soon as you wake up, take a few moments and jot down the events and key symbols from your dreams. Look up a symbol in the dictionary and review its universal meaning. Then ask yourself if the symbol contains any personal meaning beyond the universal definition appearing in the dictionary. I also encourage you to create your own dream dictionary as you progress in your dream work based on your unique beliefs and experiences. It may take weeks to fully interpret a dream, but know that devoting just a few minutes a day will eventually lead to greater awareness in your waking life. Sweet dreams.

The 10 Universal Rules of Dream Symbols

The most important concept in dream interpretation is that everyone and everything you dream about is a representation of yourself. Because no single dictionary can meet the unique needs of every dreamer, it is important to review dreams in the context of these ten rules:

Rule #1
Dreams you have about other people are actually dreams about yourself. The people in the dream represent various aspects of your personality.

Rule #2
Dreams about animals are dreams about the compulsive, habitual, or instinctual aspects of your personality.

Rule #3
The dream's setting, including environments and buildings, represent your current state of mind and attitude about the world.

Rule #4
The action that takes place in the dream is the main point of the dream.

Rule #5
Dreams about the past suggest that you are dwelling on past opportunities and are not fully engaged in the present.

Rule #6
Dreams related to the earth represent the subconscious knowledge that exists in your soul and is typically unavailable to your conscious, except in your dreams.

Rule #7
Water and its infinite variations represent your conscious mind or physical everyday knowledge.

Rule #8
Dreams about dying represent the metaphorical death of personal qualities you believe are no longer useful.

Rule #9
A journey and modes of transportation represent your movement through life.

Rule #10
Sex dreams rarely have sexual meaning. They represent aspects of your conscious and subconscious that need to be united.

An A-Z Guide to Dream Symbols

Abandon

Remember the first time you were lost in a department or grocery store? Abandonment is probably one of your earliest experiences with fear and dreams about being left behind suggest that you are feeling unloved or alone in your waking life. Dreams of abandonment may also point out your lack of independence in a current relationship. Are you relying too heavily on the person who has abandoned you in your dream? Examine the primary characteristics of the person who abandoned you and ask yourself if these qualities are represented in a person with whom you are emotionally involved. If, after introspection, you find that you are in a controlling relationship, your dream may be indicating that it is time to forge out on your own.

Abortion

Dreaming of an abortion relates to a decision that has been made regarding terminating an important project or relationship before it was complete. For example, you may have recently experienced a job loss or ended your marriage. If you haven't recently ended a project or relationship, be prepared to face a tough decision.

Accident

You may dream about being in or witnessing an accident when you are experiencing anxiety in your waking life. This type of dream is rarely a premonition. For example, if you dream about a car or airplane accident, you are simply experiencing anxiety about your own or someone else's physical well-being. Don't cancel your travel plans; confront your fears and practice in-flight yoga.

Adultery

Everyone at some time dreams about engaging in sexual acts with someone other than their mate and vice versa. If you are engaging in a midnight rendezvous, examine the qualities of your dream lover, as these are the emotional or sexual qualities that you are looking for in yourself. If you dream that your mate is having an affair, look at the qualities of his/her dream lover. Again, they are qualities you would like to develop more fully within yourself. Sex dreams are rarely wish fulfillment or premonitions, so relax and enjoy.

Airplane

A commercial airplane represents the groups of people or organizations that support you throughout your life's journey. A smooth, comfortable journey may suggest feelings of support and admiration from your colleagues whereas a plane crash may suggest anxiety about lack of support. Take some time off from work to gain a clearer perspective on your professional life as your dream is likely based on fears rather than reality.

Airport

Airports represent new beginnings and endings. If you dream that you are alone in an airport, consider whether you felt abandoned or independent. This is a good indication of your current outlook on life. Also consider the characteristics of your travel companions as they may provide clues as to the skills you will need to develop as you embark on your life's journey.

Alcohol

Dreams about drinking alcohol should alert you to the passions of your subconscious mind. As is true in waking life, your true passions are often revealed when you are inebriated. The actions and activities that take place in your dreams may suggest what you subconsciously desire in your waking life. Ask yourself, "Is this my true desire?" If the answer is "yes," then take steps toward achieving that goal in your waking life.

Alien

Dreams about aliens indicate that you are feeling like an outsider among your peers. Consider what is making you feel like an outsider. Are your thoughts and attitudes alienating you from others? Are your methods or approach different than those of others? While feeling like an outsider among your peers may leave you feeling alone and isolated, be true to your authentic self. Revealing yourself to others is accompanied by the risk of not being accepted, but it is worth the risk.

Alone

Being alone in a dream may highlight feelings of loneliness or independence depending on the context of the dream. For example, dreams of being alone in a place that is usually teeming with people, such as a shopping mall or large city, may indicate loneliness whereas being alone in nature may suggest tranquility.

Altar

An altar carries religious connotations of either sacrifice or rebirth. Either way, an event that takes place at an altar symbolizes a public announcement of your beliefs. Are you planning to announce a personal belief to family, friends, or coworkers? Are you getting married, having a baby, changing your religion, or coming out of the closet? If so, your dream is an indication that it is time to make your beliefs known.

Ambulance

Does it take a siren and flashing red lights to make you wake up and take notice of an urgent situation in your life? When an ambulance appears in your dream, it is conveying to you that this dream deals with an important issue you have been ignoring in your waking life. You may need to revisit this dream several times to uncover its meaning.

Amputation

Dreaming of amputation suggests that you are afraid to lose your power or ability in the area of your life that the amputated body part symbolizes. For example, the arms represent your ability to love and nurture. If you dream that your arms have been amputated, then you fear you have lost your ability to love. See the entry on the part of the body in question to learn more.

Angel

Angels represent guidance and the need for spiritual development. Do you know when and how to ask for the support that you need? Dreaming about angels represents your desire to connect with a spiritual teacher or guide regarding an important decision in your life. You may want to consider joining a meditation group, for example, in order to connect with like-minded individuals.

Animal

Animals are frequent visitors in dreams and they symbolize human traits and desires. Your interaction with the animals in your dreams will help you to identify your feelings about this particular characteristic or desire within yourself. See separate listings for individual animals.

Antique

Antiques symbolize your past experiences. For example, a dream about an antique bed is actually a reflection on your past sexual relationships. The fact that an antique bed appeared in your dreams indicates that you need to reexamine your past relationships in order to become involved in a fulfilling and lasting relationship.

Apartment

The rooms in an apartment represent the various aspects of your life. Unlike a house, an apartment is not composed of various levels, so the dream is likely pointing to the physical everyday aspects of your life. See separate listings for bathroom, bedroom, hall, and kitchen.

Apple

An apple represents a spiritual or intellectual beginning or awakening. Eating an apple suggests assimilating spiritual principles and peeling an apple suggests that you are cutting through layers of your personality to reveal your spiritual or intellectual core. Regardless of your religious beliefs, the apple also carries cultural connotations of original sin, so your dream may further point to those aspects of yourself that you believe to be immoral.

Apron

An apron represents the motherly or nurturing side of your personality. Regardless of whether you are a man or a woman, an apron is a reminder of the physical and emotional nourishment received in your mother's kitchen. Has someone in your life been particularly needy? Have you been clinging too closely to someone you hope can take care of you? If so, it may be time to cut the apron strings.

Arena

An arena represents an area of conflict in your life. Important and public events, such as concerts and athletic games, are held in arenas and the event in your dream will provide clues about the area of conflict. A sporting event suggests that your competitive nature is causing problems for you at work. A concert suggests that there is a problem at home.

Arm

Arms may represent either love and comfort or your ability to fight and defend yourself depending on how they are used in your dream. If you are feeling the need to love and comfort yourself or another person, your arms may be open or outstretched in your dream. If you feel the need to defend yourself in your waking life, you may fight or push people away in your dreams.

Arrest

If you dream of being arrested, you are likely struggling with a moral issue in your waking life. Guilt is a self-imposed prison and your dream suggests that you are feeling guilty about something you did or said and you are afraid of being caught. Often, the best way to end these types of dreams is to confess your crimes.

Art

If you are creating art or viewing artwork in your dream, pay close attention to the content and colors of the artwork as they represent your subconscious self-expression. For example, finger painting indicates your need to engage in more childlike behaviors and abstract art represents a desire to hide from yourself or others.

Artist

Dreaming of an artist, whether the artist is you or another person, indicates a subconscious need for self-expression. The artist represents the part of you that is creative and intuitive and may be repressed. You may need to express your creativity more outwardly through the arts in order to get in touch with your emotions.

Attic

Rooms in a house represent the body. An attic represents the mind, particularly past experiences and memories. Typical attic dreams include being chased into an attic, which represents being forced to recall past experiences, and cleaning or rummaging through an attic, which represents a desire to sort through and purge negative memories. This dream is a good indication that you need to stop living in the past.

Audience

The people in your life who objectively view your actions, such as your coworkers or your community, may be represented as audience members in your dreams. There is a public aspect of your life that is causing you concern or is capturing the attention of others, and you are feeling observed and judged.

Avalanche

Dreaming of an avalanche means that you are in danger of losing control over rapidly descending emotions. Repressed emotions, which are at the root of most catastrophic dreams, are the reason for the slide. The next time you find yourself repressing your emotions, consult a trusted friend or counselor.

Baby

Dreams about babies do not usually represent your own children. Their appearance in your dreams is typically metaphorical and represents a new project, idea or way of life. Dreaming of a baby may also represent a need for purity, innocence or nurturing.

Back

The back represents strength of character. Seeing someone else's back means that you think he disapproves of you, a crooked back represents a flawed character, and a broken back represents irrecoverable damage caused by lack of morals. Dreams about backs are often indicators of what could follow if you continue along your current path. If you change course now, you could avoid permanent damage.

Baggage

Baggage represents the emotions and memories that you carry with you over the years despite the fact that they weigh you down. When you dream of baggage, it suggests that you are still negatively affected by an event in the past and that it is time to start healing your emotional wounds.

Baker

A baker is a positive dream symbol related to creativity, productivity, or transformation. There may be an area in your life that is undergoing a period of change, and dreaming about a baker suggests that you are on the right track toward achieving your goals.

Balance

Dreams related to balance, such as walking a tightrope, indicate that you are having difficulty finding equilibrium in life. It may be time to refocus your priorities.

Balcony

If you dream that you are on a balcony it means that you are searching for power over a particular situation. Look down from your balcony to determine the area of your life that you are hoping to control. For example, watching animals from a balcony indicates a need to control your desires and watching children play represents a need to exercise reason in your life.

Bald

Ask anyone who has lost their hair and they'll likely tell you that part of their femininity, masculinity, or beauty went along with it. Dreams about baldness or losing your hair mean that you are experiencing anxiety about losing your looks or about changing your opinions and beliefs.

Ball

A ball or spherical object represents wholeness and perfection. You may believe that the pieces of your life's puzzle are falling into place and this may be represented in images of holding a ball, drawing a circle in the sand, or constructing balls out of pliable material, such as dough. Playing a ball game or throwing a ball suggests challenges, competition, and playfulness as it relates to sex.

Balloon

Quiet down Freud, we're not talking about breasts here, but feelings of joy in life. Dreams about balloons are connecting you to childlike and celebratory periods in your life. Perhaps you are feeling free-spirited and carefree lately. Enjoy it.

Band

Dreaming about an elastic band is a dream about flexibility and not setting limitations. Dreams about musical bands are about different parts of your life, such as your personality or family, working together harmoniously.

Bank

Dreams about banks relate to managing emotional and spiritual resources. If you dream about a bank robbery, you are insecure about your ability to safeguard resources for the future.

Bar

Dreams that take place in bars relate to your feelings about society or the community. For some people, bars represent relaxation and enjoyment. If this is your belief, dreaming about being in a bar can indicate a desire to relax or have fun. If bars and drinking carry negative connotations for you, the dream may represent anxiety or loneliness.

Barber

A trip to the barber represents a desire to change your opinion about yourself. These opinions may be as serious as your religious and political beliefs or as trivial as your opinion about the way you look and how you appear to the outside world.

Basement

The basement represents the emotions, traumatic events, or guilty experiences that you have repressed in waking life. Your subconscious is pulling these emotions out of storage for you to reevaluate.

Bat

Despite Hollywood's glamorization of that dark, mysterious, caped crusader, bats generally connote unknown fears; particularly fear of the subconscious mind. Baseball bats represent male sexuality and aggression.

Bath

Taking a bath represents a spiritual or emotional cleansing. It can also represent your need to cleanse yourself of guilt or "come clean." Bathing someone in your dream may represent a need to nurture that person.

Bathroom

If the dream is about the bathroom in general, it may represent a need for emotional or spiritual cleansing similar to dreaming about a bath. Dreams about toilets relate to attitudes toward privacy.

Battle

Physical battles represent struggles or conflicts in your waking life. Consider the characteristics of those battling to determine if they represent someone with whom you are struggling. As always, don't rule out the possibility that the individuals who are fighting represent different aspects of your personality that are in conflict.

Beach

Ah, the beach. The sand between your toes, the cool ocean breeze. . . standing on the border between your subconscious and conscious life. Not a typical day at the beach anymore. If you dream of the beach, a change is needed and you are standing on the threshold of that change. Take the next step.

Bear

Bears are solitary creatures that are quietly oppressive and dangerous when provoked. Sound like any female figure in your life? The bear represents overpowering parental love, usually from the mother.

Bed

Beds or bedrooms represent the private, intimate, and sexual parts of your life. Take note of the condition of the bed or bedroom. For example, if the bed is not made or the bedroom is messy it represents sexual imbalance. Is the bed too big? Perhaps sex plays too large a role in your life. If the bed is too small, then you're not sexually satisfied.

Bee

Bees can have either positive or negative connotations depending on the events that take place in the dream. If the bees were non-threatening, they may represent a productive area of your life or a difficult project you are working on with a group. Think of the orderly community of a hive. If the bees are swarming or chasing you, they represent painful or stinging emotions that you cannot escape. This may be a warning that you are soon going to be hurt by a situation that has become uncontrollable.

Beggar

When beggars manifest in your dreams, you are being confronted with feelings of failure that you are avoiding in your waking life. You may fear losing your job or not having the resources necessary to provide for yourself or your family.

Bell

This is your subconscious wake-up call. The bell may appear as a school bell, doorbell, or even an alarm. It is a warning to be cautious in your waking life because danger may lie ahead.

Belt

A man's belt represents power or authority and a woman's belt represents virtue and purity. Are you missing your belt? If so, you may believe these qualities to be absent in your life. A belt that is too tight may indicate that these qualities are constraining you.

Bicycle

Bicycles represent mobility and your life's journey, particularly the journey through childhood. As with any other object of motion, take into account its condition as well as the conditions affecting your journey.

Bird

Birds symbolize the soul or spirit. Is the bird in your dream free, caged, or flying high? This dream is an indication of your subconscious beliefs about your spirit.

Birth

If you are pregnant, dreams of giving birth are your subconscious' way of preparing for birth, or expressing anxiety about birth. If you are not pregnant, birth represents a new way of life, a new ability, or a new project.

Bite

If you bite someone in your dream, it means that you are experiencing aggression toward that person in your waking life. The reverse is true, if you are bitten. If an insect bites you, then something that has been bothering you has finally come to a head.

Black

Black represents the unknown or the subconscious. It may also represent fear, depression or death.

Blindness

Blindness represents willingness to see yourself as you truly are. Without the pretense of appearance, you are able to understand the core essence of yourself and others. You may be relying too heavily on appearances.

Blood

The blood coursing through your veins is what sustains you and gives you energy. If you are losing blood in your dream, you may be fearful of your health or believe that you are sacrificing an important aspect of yourself. Dreams that are rated "R" for violence occur because you are going through a fearful or difficult time in your life.

Blue

Light blue represents intuition, inspiration, and spirituality whereas dark blue represents disappointment or depression.

Boat

A boat represents an emotional journey, usually related to relationships. Pay particular attention to the conditions of the journey. If the ride is rocky, then you are going through a turbulent time. If you are alone on the journey, then you feel alone in one of your relationships.

Body

The body is a main source of symbolism in dreams. All that you think and feel is manifested in the body. See separate listings for individual body parts.

Bomb

A bomb represents an explosive emotional situation. Your subconscious realizes that it may only be a matter of time before your repressed emotions explode.

Book

Books represent information, knowledge, and memories. Is there something new that you need to learn? If you recall the book's title, your subconscious is telling you it is time to study that subject in your waking life. Old books represent inherited wisdom or spiritual awareness.

Boss

The boss represents authority and work. Surprisingly, you may end up taking a roll in the hay with your boss in your dreams despite the fact you may not be attracted to your boss in waking life. This is simply a dream about lack of control or power in your life.

Box

A box represents the confinement of emotions. If you are packing a box then you are unwilling to deal with your conflicted emotions.

Conversely, unpacking a box suggests a willingness to explore your emotions.

Breast

Aside from their obvious sexual connotations, breasts, particularly breast-feeding, indicate a need for nurturing or a desire to return to infancy.

Breath

Your breath represents life and the condition of your breath is a reflection of the pace of your life. Holding your breath suggests fear and anxiety, rapid breathing suggests excitement, for example. If you dream of holding your breath underwater you are fearful of your subconscious emotions.

Bride

Dreams about brides highlight your feelings about marriage. This may be an upcoming, past, or current marriage or a metaphorical marriage, such as a business merger.

Bridge

When you are transitioning from one phase of life to another, you may dream about a bridge. The condition of the bridge is a good indication of how you are reacting to the change in your life. If the bridge is secure, for example, you are feeling confident, whereas a falling bridge indicates fear.

Brown

Brown is symbolic of the earth and is associated with your physical reality.

Bubble

Bubbles represent the delicate and fragile nature of happiness and existence. If you find yourself blowing bubbles in your dream, then you are aware of the precarious nature of your happiness. True contentment lies in accepting that change is inevitable.

Building

Buildings are symbolic of the body. When attempting to interpret the meaning of a building in your dream, first consider the type of building, then the characteristics of that building. See separate entries for types of building. See also separate listings for parts of buildings.

Bull

Bulls represent your sex drive and their appearance in your dreams represents newfound confidence with your sexuality. Perhaps you are in a new relationship that has opened doors to sexual freedom.

Burglary

Dreams about burglars alert you to fears about personal safety. If you live alone, you may doubt your ability to protect yourself and your belongings. If this interpretation does not apply, ask yourself if you feel anxious about losing a part of yourself as the burglar in your dreams may be robbing you of an aspect of your personality, such as your self-esteem or identity.

Burial

You've likely whined "I'm buried alive," referring to paperwork, housework, or some other chore; being buried alive in your dreams symbolizes feeling overwhelmed by responsibility in your personal or professional life. Dreams about someone else's burial do not necessarily symbolize a physical death, but the burying of an emotion or relationship with which you have been unable to come to terms. If so, it's time to let go of the past.

Bus

This mode of public transportation represents the part of your life's journey that is accompanied by groups of people, such as family friends, or colleagues. You may be experiencing changes at work or your role in the community or within a community organization may have recently changed.

Butterfly

Butterflies symbolize positive personal transformation. Our journey toward self-awareness is marked by a prolonged metamorphosis much like that of the butterfly. Dreaming about butterflies is a reminder that although the journey may be long, the results are worth it.

Cactus

A prickly situation or person may be symbolized as a cactus in your dream. Being surrounded by cacti suggests feeling overwhelmed with difficulties.

Cage

A cage represents a loss of freedom. If you are the one caged in the dream, you are feeling trapped or restricted. Who holds the key to the cage? Remember you are often your own captor and imprison yourself with negative thoughts or emotions.

Calendar

A calendar represents the passage of time. The month depicted on the calendar may also provide clues for interpretation. The calendar may point to a month or date of a special event or it may point to your birth month, indicating your birth sign and the core characteristics of your sign.

Camera

Being photographed in your dreams means that you need to focus your attention on a particular aspect of your life. Taking pictures indicates a desire to capture a detail or event for later use.

Camp

Camping represents a temporary phase in your life. For example, if you dream of camping with your current boyfriend you subconsciously know that this relationship will be short lived.

Cancer

Dreaming that you have cancer can be frightening and may be a wake-up call that you are out of balance, physically or emotionally. There is something in your life that you are not letting go.

Candle

A candle represents clarity, hope, and a connection to the spirit. Lighting a candle means that you are shedding light on a new issue or an old issue is now clear. If the candle in the dream is burning out, you may fear aging or death.

Car

Your motivations are represented in driving a car. If you are driving, then you are in control of your life's journey. If you are a passenger, you have relinquished control of your destiny to someone else. Alone? You are independent. Did you crash the car? If so, you fear failure. If you are driving the car recklessly, you need to slow down and begin living your life more responsibly.

Carousel

A carousel, or merry-go-round, represents an aspect of your life that has no beginning or end in sight. Addictions, for example, may be represented as a carousel. Consider those aspects of your life that might be out of control.

Carpenter

Dreams that involve carpenters represent an aspect of your life that needs to be developed or restored. Notice the tools that the carpenter is using as they will add another dimension of meaning to your dream. For example, a saw represents a relationship that has been severed and a drill represents an issue that you need to delve into.

Carriage

A carriage represents your animalistic or sexual motivations along your life's journey, similar to the way that a car represents other motivations.

Castle

In fairy tales, kings and queens are protected in the security of their castles. In dreams, castles also represent safety. In addition, because this type of security is mostly afforded to important or esteemed individuals, castles, particularly if they appear palatial, suggest a desire to be important.

Cat

Cats are symbols of female sexuality, power, and independence. While the characteristics of animals in dreams can represent your own qualities or the qualities of others, cats always represent your own feline qualities.

Cave

Caves represent the female reproductive system: the womb and birth. They may also represent the subconscious, as they are dark, mysterious places.

Ceiling

A ceiling serves as protection from the stress of the outside world and its condition in your dream indicates your ability to cope with this stress. A leaking roof suggests that outside influences are infecting your thinking and may be causing negativity. It may be time to turn off the news and relax.

Celebrity

Famous people often cameo in dreams to draw attention to particular aspects of your life that need to be scrutinized. Consider the qualities that best represent the celebrity, and then determine if these are qualities that you admire or disrespect in yourself.

Cemetery

Cemeteries represent your feelings about death. If you have been recently reminded of an old trauma, you may dream of a cemetery. If someone you know is being buried, the person represents an aspect of yourself that has metaphorically been buried.

Chair

A chair represents a desire to take a rest or relax. Dreaming about a chair is a good indication that you need to reprioritize and take some time for yourself. If there are an overwhelming number of chairs in your dream or if you are constantly rearranging chairs, your life is out of control and you may want to consider an extended rest away from the chores of home life.

Chase

Being chased is a common dream theme. It represents something that you are trying to run away from in your everyday life that you fear. Pay careful attention to who is chasing you. A stranger represents you, the opposite sex represents love, and animals represent passion. Ask yourself if it is time to confront a particular fear in your life. If you have practiced lucid dreaming, try to confront the pursuer in your dreams. This is the first step toward confronting your fears and may provide you with insight on how to confront this fear in your waking life.

Child

When children appear in dreams, either known or unknown, your subconscious is asking you to pay attention to your inner child. Perhaps you need to revisit a childhood memory or issue or reexamine an area of your life that makes you feel vulnerable.

Choking

Ever choke on your own words or wish somebody else would? Choking represents an inability or difficulty expressing your emotions. Choking also suggests indecision. You may feel the need to express yourself, but you are not sure how to approach a particular topic or person. It is better to choke on your words than not utter them at all.

Church

Dream scenes that contain symbols of worship are related to religious or spiritual beliefs. Morality is the backbone of religion and dreaming about church suggests that you are searching for answers regarding your belief system.

Cigarette

Depending on whether you are a smoker, nonsmoker, or ex-smoker, smoking cigarettes can either represent pleasure or pain. Ex-smokers frequently dream about smoking as a compensatory measure since they can't smoke in their waking life.

Circle

The concepts of completeness and unity are exemplified in a circle or circular object. Dreams that contain circles indicate that you are experiencing greater awareness in your life.

City

The meaning of your dream will depend largely upon your association with the city in waking life. Even if the city is not specific, ask yourself what characteristics were most obvious about the city, as this will indicate your relationship with your own community. For example, being lost in the city may mean that you have not found your niche within your community.

Cliff

We all face times in life when decisions need to be made that can drastically change the course of our lives. Standing on a cliff represents the precarious position of having to make a choice. All decisions involve risk, and the cliff is the ultimate symbol of the danger and thrill involved in risk taking.

Climb

Life can be an upward battle, and no symbol represents this idea better than climbing. Typically, climbing represents progress or achievement of a goal, but the conditions of your climb are more important than the climb itself. Is it difficult? Are obstacles in your way?

Clock

Clocks obviously suggest time, but instruments of time are telling you more than the hour; they represent urgency and indicate a situation that needs your immediate attention. If possible, try to identify the time on the clock, as this might provide further clues about the urgent situation to which your dream is pointing.

Clothes

Clothes represent your public self and how you appear to the world. Are the clothes sexy or tattered? This is likely how you believe others see you. See separate listings for individual items of clothing.

Cloud

Clouds, because of their position among the heavens, represent the spirit. Generally, clouds are positive symbols unless they are ominous or gray, in which case they represent depression.

Coat

A coat implies that you are shielding yourself and your emotions from the outside world. As the outermost layer of clothing, a coat provides the greatest protection. Taking off a coat represents a willingness to expose your character.

Coffin

Coffins represent an ending, either physical or metaphorical. Remember, when one door closes another opens and your dream may be allowing you to gain the closure that you are unable to gain in your waking life. It may be your subconscious' subtle way of telling you to move on.

Cold

If you dream of being cold, then you are feeling neglected or isolated in your waking life. Spend time cultivating your relationship.

Color

Most people dream in color, but have difficulty recalling them. If you can remember colors, spend time exploring their meanings as they add depth to each symbol. See separate listings for individual colors.

Compass

If a compass appears in your dream, this is an indication that you are feeling lost and need to be pointed in the right direction. The north represents the unknown, the south represents your sexuality, the east represents birth, and the west symbolizes death.

Computer

In this high-tech era, computers represent information. Depending on your relationship with computers, this can be either a positive or negative symbol. For example, some people might consider their computers and the information they provide to be overwhelming and confusing because they are inundated with work files and e-mails. For others, computers may represent an exciting connection to the world.

Cooking

Cooking represents a subconscious desire to nourish your creativity. Take an art class, get back to nature, write poetry, or try your hand in the kitchen.

Corner

Dreaming about a corner indicates that you have reached a critical point in your life. If you find yourself facing a corner in your dream, you may feel like you are trapped in your waking life. Of course there are always two ways to turn out of a corner. You must choose a new direction to continue to grow.

Cow

Cows are positive dream symbols. Their passivity and domesticity are reminders of motherhood and represent nourishment or fertility.

Crowd

Crowds represent how you relate to groups of people. Do crowds provide you with a feeling of belonging or do they overwhelm you?

Crown

A crown represents status and success. Wearing a crown in your dreams may be your subconscious pat on the back for a successful job that you recently completed. Perhaps you have experienced recognition at work or at home and the crown is a symbol of your increased status.

Crying

Crying is a reminder to release pent up emotions. If you are holding back sorrow, pain, anger, or frustration, have a good cry in your waking life and consider yourself cleansed.

Cutting

To interpret your dream, consider whether you were cutting to destroy or create. Cutting to sever an object represents severing emotions or relationships that are no longer useful. For example,

Cutting

cutting clothes may mean abandoning a façade that is no longer necessary. However, cutting as it relates to creating, such as cutting a pattern or creating a collage, suggests creativity.

Dam

Dams represent repressed emotions. For example, are you building the dam or is it being torn down? Is the dam leaking?

Dance

Dancing is your subconscious' way of exaggerating your emotions, and the manner of dancing indicates the mood. For example, ecstatic hip-hop dancing represents joy, slow dancing represents sexuality, and ballet represents discipline.

Danger

Danger appears in dreams when you are facing anxiety in your waking life. Danger can appear in many forms, such as fires, floods, or physical terror.

Dark

The dark represents the subconscious or hidden side of your personality. The fact that you are dreaming about the dark is an indication that you want to explore this side of your personality. Too many people ignore the aspects of themselves that they believe to be negative, but you must know your whole self in order to achieve self-awareness.

Dawn

Dawn or early morning represents hope. New beginnings, such as marriage, the birth of a child, or your own spiritual rebirth may be represented in dreams of dawn or a sunrise. This dream is a celebration of your new beginning.

Death

People appear in your dreams to reveal aspects of yourself; therefore, when someone dies in your dream ask yourself what is coming to an end in your life? Dreams about death typically occur during periods of transitions, such as getting married, divorcing, or becoming a mother.

Deer

Deer represent what is gentle and defenseless in this world. These characteristics may be present in you or someone close to you.

Demolition

Dreaming of demolition, such as a car demolition or derby, represents a need for power or control. Are you watching the destruction or participating?

Descending

Dreams that involve descending represent a downward progression or lack of progress in life. You may feel that your life is going nowhere, and that any step you take forward only leads to two steps back; this is represented either by falling or walking downward.

Desert

Because deserts are dry, relatively lifeless expanses, they are associated with feelings of emptiness or abandonment. Unless, of course, you grew up in or enjoy vacationing in a desert region, in which case the desert will have positive connotations.

Desk

Your desk represents your work life, particularly the day-to-day tasks. Is it crowded and messy? If so, you are feeling overwhelmed at work. An empty desk suggests that you are not feeling utilized. You may be going through a period of professional transition and anxiety related to work that is manifesting itself in your dream. If this image recurs, examine your workload objectively, then have a heart to heart with your boss.

Diamond

The marketing geniuses in the diamond industry have taught us that "diamonds are forever" and culturally they are believed to represent beauty and purity. Because they are the gemstone of choice for engagements, they also represent everlasting love. Their appearance in dreams represents something worth treasuring.

Digging

Since you have begun monitoring and interpreting your dreams, you are uncovering aspects of yourself previously concealed and this is often represented in dreams related to digging a hole or digging for an item.

Dinosaur

Dinosaurs are ancient creatures that represent archaic beliefs. Are you living in the past? Do you maintain or perpetuate beliefs related to racism or sexism that are now extinct? It is difficult to abandon deeply ingrained beliefs, but necessary for continued survival.

Dirt

Dirt may appear in your dreams when it is necessary for you to connect with your subconscious instincts and desires no matter how unpleasant. You may be feeling physically or mentally polluted and you need to get to the root of your negative thoughts and attitudes.

Disguise

Since clothing represents how you appear to the outside world, wearing a disguise represents your desire to hide yourself or your emotions from others. The type of disguise may further reveal the emotions you are attempting to hide. For example, wearing a mask suggests a desire to reveal your identity and a hat represents a desire to reveal your role in life, such as your role of spouse or employee.

Diving

Diving dreams represent delving into the subconscious or unknown areas of your life and personality. Your feelings associated with the dive relate to your feelings about exploring your subconscious. For example, was the exploration anxiety provoking because you did not know how to swim or could not breathe? Or, was the dive exciting and full of pleasant discovery?

Divorce

Dreaming about divorce may be interpreted literally to mean that you have a fear or hope of ending your marriage. Divorce dreams may also represent a more symbolic end to a project or phase of life.

Doctor

Doctors represent something in your life that needs healing. Is the doctor in your dream a surgeon? Perhaps something needs to be physically removed from your life. If the doctor appears as a psychiatrist, your mental health needs to be examined.

Dog

Just ask my four-legged friend—dogs represent loyalty and unconditional love. However, if you have experienced a negative canine encounter in the past, dogs may represent aggression.

Doll

Dolls represent your childlike nature or an underdeveloped aspect of your personality. Ask your parents what you were like as a child. As we mature, we often forget about our childhood hobbies or inclinations. Once uncovered, you may notice that an important aspect of yourself has been lost over the years.

Donkey

Donkeys represent stubbornness or a burden. Riding a donkey indicates a desire to maintain your position. Walking in front of or alongside of a donkey suggests a burden you carry with you whereas walking behind a donkey suggests an inability to move beyond your burden.

Door

If the door in the dream is open, then an opportunity has presented itself to you. You may need to be more open to new possibilities or people or you may be entering a new phase of life. Closed doors represent a phase of your life that has been completed.

Dragon

Dragons represent physical power and sexual energy. Dreaming about dragons is a reminder to manage these sometimes frightening aspects of your own life.

Dress

If you are wearing a dress in your dream, your subconscious is bringing your feminine qualities to your attention. Perhaps you have not been exercising your feminine qualities and they may be helpful in solving a particular problem.

Drink

Dreams about drinking may be compensatory. You may need to let loose or indulge in your waking life. No, this is not a green light to bar crawl, just a reminder to celebrate life. Also consider that you may dream about drinking because you are physically thirsty. You may dream about a glass of water, for example, and the urge to drink will be so strong that you will wake up.

Driving

Driving dreams are similar to car dreams in that they represent the manner in which you are controlling your life. You're in the driver's seat—how are you handling the road? Are you driving cautiously? Is your foot on the accelerator but you are not moving? Are you driving recklessly?

Drowning

Drowning symbolizes an overwhelming aspect of your life that makes you feel suffocated or helpless. If you are feeling overwhelmed by emotions, you may dream about drowning. This dream is a good indication that you need to examine the stress in your life.

Drum

A drum represents a heartbeat and the natural rhythms of our lives. If drums are playing in the background, you should feel confident that the dream theme is a healthy and natural one. If you are beating a drum, then you are in tune with the rhythms of your life.

Dwarf

Is there an aspect of your life that you feel is underdeveloped? For example, have you spent so much time managing your career that you have neglected to develop your personal relationships? Have you cared for others more than you have cared for yourself?

Ear

There is a direct correlation between the physical and symbolic purpose of the ears—to listen. If emphasis is placed on this body part in your dream, it may mean that you need to listen more carefully or pay more attention to a particular aspect of your life that has been neglected.

Earth

Earth represents stability and solidity and may symbolize a need to be grounded. Culturally, earth is represented as female and may further represent your maternal nature or desire to be mothered.

Earthquake

Natural disasters usually represent extreme emotions; however, earthquakes represent the physical self. Usually, earthquake dreams are caused by a physical or financial upset in your life that is causing you to feel uncertain.

Eating

You eat in your dreaming life for many of the same reasons you eat in waking life—to nourish your body and often your psychological and spiritual needs. If you are overeating in your dream, you are stuffing down your emotions. If you are malnourished, then you do not love yourself, because you are rejecting growth or change. If you are baking an apple pie for an ex-lover in your dreams, then you have been giving too freely of yourself.

Egg

Eggs are feminine dream symbols that often appear when you are questioning or exploring your desire to have children. Eggs represent prenatal life and the hope that comes with the potential of new life. Eating an egg suggests embracing new life and breaking an egg suggests confusion about reproductive choices.

Elephant

Elephants represent power and patience and are positive dream symbols related to success. Dreaming about elephants is often related to your memory and the subconscious may be tying a ribbon around your finger to help you remember an important event.

Elevator

Life is full of ups and downs and what better symbol than an elevator to represent these emotions? Unlike the symbols tied to ascending or descending, the symbol of an elevator represents emotions moving quickly and often from one extreme to the other. And, don't be surprised if your elevator dreams are sexual in nature.

Escape

Dreams about escaping are dreams about running away from your fears and often involve pursuit. Consider what you need to face in life. This can be something as inconsequential as a project you've been putting off or as significant as losing someone who is close to you.

Either way, the only way to end your nocturnal escapades is to confront your fears in waking life.

Examination

Dreaming of taking an exam along with some variation of not being prepared for the exam is a typical anxiety dream. Perfectionism is rearing its ugly head even in your dream world. Fear of failing and not living up to your own high self-standards is keeping you in your high school science classroom.

Ex-Boyfriend/Girlfriend/Husband/Wife

Haven't you learned your lessons from that relationship yet? When The Ex appears in your dream, it is because you still have lessons to learn from that relationship or there are old issues that need to be worked out before you can truly move forward. These dreams are common and can bring greater depth and understanding to your current relationship, if you are willing to examine them.

Explosion

An explosion suggests extreme emotion. For example, an explosion may represent rage in a dream that deals with an issue with which you are dissatisfied or it may represent an orgasm in an erotic dream.

Eye

Eyes allow you to view the world, and when you dream about eyes or eyesight it is an indication that there is something in your life that needs to be examined more carefully.

Face

Strange and familiar faces make up your dreams. Not surprising, considering the people in your dreams represent aspects of yourself—you are a complex and multi-faceted individual. When the emphasis in the dream is on the individual's face more than the whole person, it represents how you express your feelings or how you believe others see you. Jung believed that the stranger, a common character in dreams, represents a part of you that is only known to the subconscious. If a faceless character appears, be patient. Subconsciously, you are aware that you are not prepared to meet this side of yourself yet.

Falling

Falling dreams are so common entire books could be devoted to their variations and interpretations. The most important point to remember about falling dreams is that they represent an aspect of your life that is out of control. Descending represents a gradual downward progression; falling dreams are sudden and frightening. In fact, you almost always wake up before hitting bottom out of actual fear.

Family

There is one exception to the rule regarding dreams about other people and that is dreams about family. Rather than representing an aspect of you, family members represent how you handle your relationships. For example, dreams about your mother represent your nurturing or feminine qualities in relationships, whereas dreams about your father represent your power or authority in your relationships. Dreams about spouses represent how you view your sexual relationships.

Farm

You may daydream about a simpler life without cell phones, high speed Internet, and a long commute. Dreaming about a farm or farmer represents the simple, natural lifestyle you may crave from time to time. Just remember that this grass is always greener on the other side and this dream is not an indication to turn in your briefcase for a backhoe, but to slow down and spend some time focused on the simpler things in life.

Fat

Society has a huge preoccupation with body image and material possessions and dreaming about fat represents your fears about your body image. Don't allow this symbol to intensify an already existing body image issue. Acknowledge the anxiety and consider hitting the treadmill five additional minutes each day.

Father

The masculine characteristics inherent in your relationships are reflected in dreams about your father. This is less a dream about you and more a dream about how you relate to other people. Your father's primary traits or those he exhibits in your dream are indicators of the attributes that you need to more carefully examine in your current relationships. In general, dreams involving your father relate to authority and power in your current relationships.

Feather

Feathers have a captivating quality because of their connection to floating and flying and represent your spiritual or emotional self. If someone gives you a feather, they should be considered an integral part of your personal development in waking life.

Female

All women in your dreams represent an aspect of yourself whether you are a man or a woman. During your dream an aspect of yourself will be revealed to you through this woman. What are her primary characteristics? For example, woman may represent intuition, nurturing, creativity, and receptiveness. Consider the predominant traits of the woman and ask yourself how they relate to your own life and current situation.

Fence

Fences are boundaries or barriers that protect you from danger. They may represent the need for privacy or defensiveness toward something or someone that you fear. Examine what is on the other side of the fence to uncover your anxiety.

Field

A field represents an activity in life, such as work, study, or a hobby. An empty field suggests a lack of activity and loneliness. A field full of people or objects may either represent a full life or one that is overfilled with commitments.

Fighting

Fighting, whether physical or verbal, represents a conflict in your life, usually with an aspect of yourself. What are the main characteristics of the person with whom you are fighting? A situation may have forced you to recently confront this aspect of yourself. If you are unable to fight back in your dream, you are feeling helpless.

Finding

Losing an important object is a common and often unsettling dream theme that suggests you have lost a part of yourself. Finding that item, on the other hand, represents a moment of enlightenment.

Finger

Your fingers represent your ability to perceive and grasp emotion. Through touch and gesture you express love with your hands, particularly your fingers. It is believed each finger is symbolic of a different emotion: thumb, your feelings about success and failure; index finger, your feelings of guilt and blame; middle finger, feelings about anger and resentment; ring finger, feelings about love and relationships; pinky finger, fear of failure.

Fire

Fire is a powerful force that may represent danger because of its destructive nature. However, since we have learned to control fire, it has provided us with warmth and passion and may also represent love. What makes fire such a powerful symbol is its ability to also represent spiritual transformation. Just as the phoenix rose out of the ashes, so does purification and new life result from a fire that has been controlled and then extinguished.

Fish

Fish represent subconscious emotions and your emotional journey through life. Catching fish may either represent coming to terms with your emotions or the death of a particular emotion. Freshwater fish, such as catfish and trout, suggest everyday emotions and a tranquil journey, whereas saltwater fish or crustaceans represent repressed emotions and a more difficult journey.

Flag

Flags represent beliefs related to patriotism, community and the nation. Waving a flag indicates a desire to make your political beliefs known, whereas a dirty or torn flag represents a confusion or breakdown in beliefs. Often, upsets in government or war will cause you to question your political beliefs.

Fly

Flies symbolize feelings of annoyance or disruption in your waking life. There may be an issue that is bothering you that you subconsciously realize will not go away unless you deal with it.

Floating

Floating is a pleasurable dream theme that represents a desire for freedom. It is a taste of happiness and lightheartedness that you may not experience in waking life. Unlike flying, floating is a passive activity that suggests you are not in complete control over your own freedom at this time. Be patient, one day soon you will be flying high!

Flood

Since water represents conscious experiences and emotions, a flood symbolizes overwhelming emotions that could result in disaster.

These are usually the seemingly inconsequential emotions of everyday life involving disappointment or work-related stress that if left unchecked can get out of hand.

Floor

Your core beliefs are reflected in the condition of the floor in your dreams. A dirty floor represents confusion and lack of purity and broken floorboards suggest an error in thinking or judgment. You will rarely dream of perfectly clean floors as your subconscious usually points out your fears rather than your accomplishments.

Flower

Flowers represent new life and growth. Notice the colors of the flowers in your dream and their condition as well as your attitude toward them. Flowers are a positive symbol of growth, so even if the flowers are wilted, it is simply an indication that you need to spend more time tending to your personal development.

Flying

Flying is an expression of personal freedom. You may have recently freed yourself from personal limitations of the mind, such as stagnant thinking or from physical limitations, such as sexual repression. Either way, flying is an indication that you have broken out of a negative and potentially destructive pattern.

Fog

Fog hinders your ability to see clearly and in dreams represents a lack of clarity in thinking. Have you been focusing too intently on only one area in your life and not seeing the big picture? Or, have you been distracted by outside influences?

Following

If you are playing follow the leader in your dreams this is an indication that you are lacking identity or confidence and are looking toward another person to guide you. Being followed in a dream represents an emotion or fear that is still with you in your waking life despite the fact that you believe you have left it behind.

Food

The appearance of food in dreams represents a desire for emotional or spiritual nourishment. This nourishment may come in the form of love or knowledge. Your relationship to the food, whether you ignore it, taste it, or overindulge in it is a good indicator of your current level of neediness.

Foot

Feet represent movement through life and dreams about feet relate to your attitude about where you are going. Are your feet firmly grounded? Are you trying to walk or run, but are unable to move? Are they pointed in the right direction?

Foreign Place

If your dream takes place in a foreign country, examine your feelings about that particular location. Your feelings about the country and its people will indicate your sentiments about the events that took place in the dream. For example, if you honeymooned in Paris, the city may evoke feelings of happiness and romance for you and dreaming of this location indicates that your dream carries romantic overtones.

Forest

A forest represents the unknown or your subconscious. Trees represent life; therefore, a forest represents the many unexplored facets of your life. If you are lost in the woods, you may feel over-whelmed and confused about the many different directions you can take in life.

Fountain

A fountain represents the emotions that you share with the world, usually those emotions related to love, passion, sexuality, and birth. Because a fountain is a public display, its appearance in dreams represents a desire to make your emotions known.

Fox

A fox represents the cunning aspects of your personality. Perhaps you subconsciously believe that you have acted in an underhanded manner in your waking life. Or you may wish to deceive or mislead someone and you are feeling anxious about the possible outcome.

Frog

Frogs represent the ability you have to transform your life. You may remember the childhood stories of the princess who took a chance and kissed the ugly frog. Of course, her ability to ignore the frog's homely appearance rewarded her with a handsome prince.

Funeral

Funerals symbolize the termination of a relationship, project, emotion, or period in your life. Has an important relationship recently terminated? Are you entering a new phase of life?

Furniture

Furniture represents your private home life and its condition represents how well you are tending to your family relationships. See separate listings for individual pieces.

Gamble

If you are playing the Vegas tables in your dream world, you are likely going through a life experience that involves risk. Your dream is a dry run for how you might handle the situation in waking life. Are you winning or losing?

Game

How well do you play the game of life? Your dreams will tell you through the types of games you play in and how well you play them. First, identify the type of game you are playing. Cards and board games, for example, typically represent strategy, whereas group games, such as sports, represent competitiveness. Notice if you are winning, losing, or cheating in the game.

Garage

Garages represent your drive, energy, and motivation. If the garage is empty, you may not feel that you have the resources to move forward in life. If the garage is overcrowded, you may feel distracted and unable to sort through your various emotions. Ask yourself how well you are maintaining these important resources in your waking life.

Garbage

What emotions or possessions are you carrying with you that have become unnecessary? Your outdated attitudes or negative feelings that need to be discarded are represented in the objects you throw in the trash in your dreams. For example, if the garbage is food waste there is something in your life that no longer nourishes you. If you are throwing away clothes, then you need to discard the guise you project to the outside world to keep people from seeing your authentic self.

Garden

Gardens represent your inner life and indicate that you are attempting to grow or transform. The condition of the garden is worth noting. For example, if you are pulling weeds, it represents freeing yourself from negative thoughts; watering the garden represents cultivating emotions.

Gate

Gates represent a passage from one phase of life to another. If the gate is open, then there is an opportunity ahead of you that must be met. A closed gate represents an external barrier keeping you from entering the next phase of your life.

Ghost

Since all the people in your dreams represent aspects of yourself, ghosts represent aspects of your past that are continuing to haunt you. You may be harboring old hurts, angers, or resentments that manifest as ghost-like figures in your dreams. Dreams about ghosts can often become nightmares if the old resentments are not dealt with in your waking life.

Giant

Who is the giant in your dream and what aspect of yourself does this person represent? Your dream is helping you understand that this feeling, fear, or emotion has grown too large and you are having difficulty handling it. For example, has an addiction become out of control?

Gift

Exchanging gifts represents the valuable emotional or spiritual aspects of self that you give to others. Who is receiving the gift? Are you giving graciously or against your will? Answering these questions will provide information on how you give and receive.

Glass

Glass represents a barrier, but because you can see through it, the dream is acknowledging that the problem you see through the glass can be observed and, therefore, conquered. Shattering glass represents a desire to break through the barriers that exist between you and a problem.

Glasses

Glasses represent how you look at the world. Typically, glasses allow you to see more clearly, but if the glasses in your dream are broken or clouded, you may have a distorted sense of reality. Sunglasses are an exception, because they indicate a desire to hide from others.

Glove

Gloves protect your hands from the elements. Since hands connect you to your surroundings and are used to express emotions, such as anger and love, you may need to protect yourself from these extreme emotions.

Goat

Goats represent the aspects of your sexuality related to your drive, determination, and tenacity. If your sex life has been less than extraordinary, but has recently received a welcome jolt due to your own assertiveness and perseverance, you may dream about a goat.

Gold

The color gold in dreams represents healing and warmth and is usually represented as an aura or halo. Gold as a currency represents what you consider valuable.

Grass

Grass represents personal growth. Are you looking over the fence at your neighbor's grass? Then you may be paying too careful attention to the activities of others and not enough attention to your personal growth. If the grass needs to be mowed, then your emotions may be getting out of hand and hindering your ability to grow. A well-manicured lawn, on the other hand, suggests contentment and sustained personal growth.

Grave

Graves represent feelings related to death. If someone has recently passed away, the dream may uncover your unresolved feelings about that person. If you see the name on the grave, consider the major attributes of that person as the grave may represent that aspect of yourself that has died.

Green

Traditionally, green represents harmony and balance within the world. However, green may also symbolize money or envy.

Grey

Grey provides a solemn tone to dreams and suggests that the dream's content is serious.

Guitar

Music is the backdrop of life and significant events are often associated with particular songs or instruments. The type of music created by the guitar is an indicator of its symbolism in the dream. Music may also represent a need for harmony in your life. Playing a guitar represents creativity.

Gun

Guns are aggressive and typically masculine symbols that relate to fear and power. If the gun is pointed at you, you feel threatened by an aggressive and masculine figure in waking life. If you are holding the gun, you may feel the need to control a threatening person or situation in your life.

Hair

Bad hair can ruin an otherwise good day. It's not surprising, considering that for most people hair represents sexuality and youthfulness. Dreaming of losing your hair represents a loss of this sexuality and cutting hair represents a change in this area of your life. If you are combing your hair, there may be unresolved sexual issues that need to be untangled. Hair may also represent your conscious thoughts or attitudes.

Hall

Hallways represent a transition from one stage of your life to another. If you are simply walking through a hall in your dream, you are aware of transitioning but unsure about the outcome. Entering a specific room will indicate the direction you believe you are headed in life.

Hammer

A hammer may either imply building or destroying depending on the events in the dream. In some instances, a hammer is an aggressive symbol of destruction. You may wish to break down an attitude, belief, or barrier in your waking life. On the other hand, the hammer may symbolize your ability to construct or mend relationships or situations.

Hand

Hands are the most dreamed of part of the body, because we use them to express our deepest emotions, such as love and fear, in our waking life. If you talk with your hands in your waking life, you probably do so in your dreams. If you recall hand gestures in your dream, consider the significance of these gestures in waking life. For example, a clenched fist suggests aggression, outstretched hands suggest a desire to connect, and clasped hands represent a partnership or friendship.

Handcuff

Being handcuffed suggests that you feel sexually restrained in waking life. Handcuffing someone else suggests a desire to control the person you are handcuffing. You are likely playing sexual games in your waking life that you find equally exciting and constraining. Know that this relationship is likely short-lived.

Hanging

Hanging onto an object, such as a cliff or ledge, represents a fear of failure. Dreams about being hung represent a desire to release a part of you that the person being hung represents. Because hangings often took place in public, dreaming of a hanging indicates that we want others to acknowledge our transformation.

Hat

Hats represent the many authoritarian roles you play in life. The type of hat represents the role that you are assigning to yourself in life. For example, if you are wearing a hood, the dream is focusing on a role you play in life related to deceit. If you are wearing a top hat, your dream is emphasizing the formal or pretentious roles you may play.

Head

The head represents the thinking or intellectual aspects of you. If your head is covered, you may be hiding your intellect. Dreams about a head injury suggest feelings of inadequacy related to intellect. For example, you may have recently failed a test or you may be having difficulty completing a project.

Heart

The heart represents love, compassion, and sensitivity. It is a vulnerable organ and dreaming about it is an acknowledgement of your own vulnerability. Individuals who have had health issues related to the heart may also dream about this part of the body due to a hyperawareness of this vital life organ.

Heat

As you continue to practice dream interpretation, paying attention to subtle nuances in your dreams, such as temperature, can add layers of meaning to your dreams. Heat may either lend a suffocating or uncomfortable tone to the dream or a passionate tone, depending on the situation.

Heaven

Regardless of your religious orientation, you may hope for the existence of utopia either in this life or the next. Dreams of heaven-like locations represent hope for happiness and peace on earth or in the afterlife.

Hell

Dreaming about a demonic underworld represents feelings of guilt, pain or fear in your life. You are likely going through a period of great difficulty.

Hero

Dreaming of a hero, such as a fireman, policeman, or other do-gooder, represents your own desire to be courageous. You may be confronted with a difficult situation in your waking life that calls on your courage of the heart or spirit and you are subconsciously struggling with the morality of this issue.

Hiding

People hide when they do not want to confront someone or something in their life. Consider the primary characteristic of the person you are hiding from in your dream. For example, if you are running from your stockbroker, who you believe to exhibit qualities of greed, you may be hoarding resources you should be sharing in your waking life.

Hill

A hill represents a surmountable challenge in your life. If you dream of climbing a hill, you have a personal goal to achieve in your life that you are working toward. If you are climbing with another person, then you share a common goal. Consider the condition of your climb, as it will indicate your feelings toward your ability to meet your goal. Standing on top of a hill symbolizes that you have achieved perspective on your goal.

Hole

A hole represents the unknown or the subconscious. Are you stuck in a hole, such as a well? You may feel that you have entered unknown emotional territory in your waking life and you don't know how to resolve your emotions. Is an animal hiding in a hole? Consider the attributes of the animal, as they are likely characteristics or habits that you are trying to hide.

Homosexuality

Dreaming about being attracted to someone of the same gender or engaging in sexual acts with someone of the same gender does not mean that you are gay. Unless you are homosexual or have recently been struggling with your sexual identity, homosexual dreams should be interpreted as your subconscious' need to embrace or come to terms with a feminine or masculine aspect of yourself that the sex partner represents.

Horse

Horses represent strength, stamina, and speed. The fact that you are dreaming about horses is a good indication that you recognize their attributes in yourself. Because they are powerful animals, they also represent intense energy. If you dream of horseback riding, you are experiencing control in your waking life. Dreaming of being thrown from a horse suggests that you feel that your life is out of control.

Hospital

Hospitals suggest a need for physical or spiritual healing. Pay careful attention to clues that might identify the area of practice. For example, dreaming of a cardiac unit suggests the need to heal wounds caused by past lovers and the emergency room suggests the need for urgent healing.

Hotel

Hotels represent a period of transition in your life. You may not realize a current period of your life as impermanent, but your subconscious does. Perhaps you are in a volatile relationship or you are feeling unappreciated at work. Dreaming about a hotel indicates that you realize that the position or relationship is short-lived.

House

A house represents the different aspects or activities in your life and the rooms are organized in a similar fashion as your body. See separate listings for attic, basement, bathroom, bedroom, hall and kitchen.

Hunger

Experiencing hunger indicates a desire for emotional nourishment in your waking life. Pay attention to how you attend to the hunger in your dreams. Overeating suggests burying emotions, whereas deprivation indicates that you have cut yourself off from the people who provide the greatest emotional support.

Hunt

Being hunted indicates that you are going through a period in your life marked by uncertainty and fear. If you are the hunter, you have recently become too egotistic in your waking life. If the hunt is not dangerous, but more hide-and-seek-related, the dream may symbolize a recent sexual pursuit.

Hurricane

Dreaming about natural disasters, such as hurricanes, suggests that you are going through a disturbing period in your life. You fear that the situation may spiral out of control and destroy the things that are most important to you. Has a situation recently escalated at home or at work? Has a small problem recently intensified?

Ice

Your everyday life experiences, particularly emotions, often materialize as water in your dreams. Therefore, dreaming of ice indicates hardened or repressed emotions. Melting ice suggests a gradual release of emotion and a desire to confide in others. Ice may also symbolize loneliness or isolation as these feelings often follow when you keep your emotions bottled inside. Your dream is an indication to share your feelings with those you trust.

Ice Cream

Eating ice cream is a pleasurable experience that may remind you of childhood. Eating ice cream in your dream means that you are accepting pleasure, particularly sexual pleasure, in your life. Giving or feeding someone else ice cream suggests that you desire to give sexual pleasure to that individual.

Igloo

An igloo represents a refuge from what you believe to be an otherwise cold and unloving environment. Despite the fact that this is not the most comfortable or luxurious home, you should be comforted knowing that you have shelter during this presumably difficult period in your life.

Illness

If you dream of your own illness, your subconscious may be reminding you to take care of your emotional and physical well-being. You've likely been burning the candle at both ends and you need to take some time for yourself. If you dream that a loved one is ill, you may fear losing that person. Consider the support that they provide you and try to further develop those qualities within yourself.

Injection

Injections suggest that you are feeling controlled or invaded by external influences. If a doctor is nurse is administering the shot, you may feel that you are not in control of your own health and healing. If someone from your daily life, such as a friend or family member, gives you a shot, consider if their opinions or attitudes are influencing you in waking life. You may want to distance yourself from that individual for a short period in order to regain your strength.

Insect

Insects indicate that something is "bugging" you in your waking life. The size of the bug may indicate the degree of annoyance. See separate entries for bee, butterfly, fly and spider.

Invisible

If you dream of being invisible, there is a part of you that is feeling ignored. You may feel unacknowledged, underappreciated, or generally alone in your waking life. Don't wait for others to take notice. You may need to remind others of your accomplishments and skills in order to regain your confidence.

Island

Dreaming about being alone on an island represents feelings of loneliness and isolation. Since water represents the conscious, an island may also represent an acknowledgment or rise in consciousness. If you dream of an island vacation, you may be in need of a vacation.

Jail

If you dream of being imprisoned, you are feeling guilty about something you have said or done in your waking life. You believe that your actions or words were immoral and you likely feel that your peers will judge you. Sometimes the best way to break out of your personal prison is to come clean. You are often your own worst critic.

Journey

All journeys represent your life's journey and paying attention to the mode of transportation, condition of travel, and travel companions should supply you with additional clues as to the meaning of your dream. For example, do you have adequate means of transportation? Is the journey pleasurable or difficult? Are you the passenger or driver?

Judge

Dreaming about a judge indicates feelings of guilt. Are you judging yourself for something you have done in your past? Have you forgiven yourself? Unlike dreams about juries that suggest outside judgment, dreams about judges indicate that you are facing your toughest critic—yourself.

Jumping

Jumping up may indicate a desire to reach a goal you believe is unattainable. Jumping downward represents impulsiveness and taking a risk. Jumping may also represent acting without thinking in your waking life. Have you made any impulsive decisions lately related to attaining a goal?

Jungle

Dreams related to jungles suggest adventure and self-discovery. Time spent in a jungle can be exciting and represent new areas of your life that you are exploring. If the safari is difficult and you find you're tangled by overgrown branches and vines and pursued by wild animals, your journey of self-discovery is anxiety-producing and overwhelming.

Jury

Juries represent your moral consciousness. If you dream of being judged by a jury you feel that others are judging you. Unlike a judge, jury members are made up of your peers and their judgment is particularly difficult to bear. Dreams about juries are particularly critical and usually ridiculous—a reminder that outside criticism is often unreasonable.

Kangaroo

Kangaroos are extremely swift and agile despite their apparent awkwardness. When kangaroos appear in your dreams, your subconscious is alerting you to your ability to move ahead. Kangaroos further suggest safety and nurturing, because of the unique manner in which they transport their young.

Key

Keys represent solutions to barriers in your life. If you are entering a new phase of life, you may see yourself standing in front of a door in your dreams. Holding keys indicates your ability to remove obstacles standing between you and the next stage of life. If you find yourself unable to unlock the door or locate the correct key, you believe that you are unable to enter the next phase of your life.

Kicking

Kicking is an aggressive dream symbol and suggests an unresolved conflict between the individuals involved in the kicking. Consider the primary attributes of the person you are kicking as more often than not the other individual represents an aspect of yourself that you are battling. Kicking is also a childlike response, and further indicates confronting childish emotions, such as jealousy or revenge.

Kidnap

If you dream that you are kidnapped, you are afraid of losing a part of yourself or of being taken away from the surroundings that comprise your identity. You may be experiencing a period of extreme happiness or comfort that you believe is too good to be true. Often people's identity is connected to material objects, such as houses and cars, and this may also be revealed in your dream.

Killing

Killing represents a part of you that is being denied or destroyed. Review the characteristics of the individuals being killed for clues as to the part of your life that is coming to an end.

King

Kings represent patriarchal power and dreaming about them suggests that you are dealing with the issue of authority in your life. Who holds the power in the royal kingdom of your dreams? Is the king someone you know? Do his qualities point to someone in your life who has authority over you, such as your boss or parent? Are you the subject, trusted confidant, or court jester?

Kissing

Kissing represents love, union, and transformation. If you have a romantic interest in the person you are kissing, the dream may depict your desire to connect with that person. If, on the other hand, you are not attracted to the person you are kissing, the person may represent an aspect of your personality that you need to learn to embrace.

Kitchen

Having a dream that takes place in a kitchen suggests that you are in need of emotional nourishment. Kitchens are further associated with women and domesticity and their appearance in dreams indicates a desire to be nurtured by those qualities typically considered to be feminine.

Kite

Kites represent elevated emotions. If you dream of flying a kite, you are celebrating your happiness in waking life while simultaneously acknowledging the precariousness of your contentment. Don't over-analyze this dream. Simply enjoy it.

Knee

Kneeling is a symbol of humility and dependence. Who are you kneeling before? Do you feel subordinate to that person in your waking life? Does your dependence on that person often leave you feeling vulnerable? Because humility and dependence are emotional responses related to your ego, this dream is an indication that you are wrestling with these issues in your waking life.

Knife

A knife is a symbol of aggressiveness and anger and its appearance in dreams indicates that someone has hurt you with painful words or actions. Unlike other aggressive actions, such as kicking or hitting, stabbing implies the potential for a much deeper wound. It may be time to sever ties with someone in your life who is causing you pain.

Knitting

Knitting is a domestic activity often equated with motherhood. If you dream about knitting, it indicates your desire to give life to a new relationship. This new beginning can be the birth of a child, a new love, or the resurrection of a current relationship.

Knock

A knock, typically at a door, symbolizes an opportunity. Pay attention to who or what is on the other side of the door, as it may suggest your destiny. If the object or person who initiated the knock causes feelings of pain or fear, the knock may also be a warning.

Knot

A knot represents a problem you are having with a relationship. Dreaming about tying a knot suggests that you feel responsible for the problems in your relationship. Dreaming of trying to untie a knot indicates a desire to resolve the emotional issues that are keeping you from attaining intimacy.

Ladder

Dreaming about climbing a ladder suggests that you are making incremental progress toward a personal or professional goal. The ladder represents a goal that you may consider unattainable and the rungs represent the steps necessary to attain the goal. This dream is a reminder that if you continue your steady progress you will attain your goal.

Lake

Water represents your conscious life experiences, particularly emotions. Lakes relate to your romantic emotions. Consider the condition of the water and your ability to stay afloat, as these are indicators of your attitude toward your current romance.

Lamb

A lamb represents the gentle and innocent side of your nature. The lamb is a powerful symbol that also indirectly points to your evil or cunning side. Your dream is acknowledging the often conflicting aspects of your personality.

Language

Language represents your ability to communicate. A dream that contains language you do not know indicates something within you that you do not understand. If you are speaking in your dream, but no one understands your words, you may feel misunderstood in your waking life.

Late

Dreaming of being late is an anxiety dream related to feeling unprepared for an upcoming event. Once you determine the upcoming event that is causing anxiety, ask yourself why you feel unprepared. Are there steps you can take that will alleviate your fear?

Laugh

Laughter typically suggests happiness and lack of inhibition. Dreaming about laughter may suggest that you need to relax or release tension in your waking life. However, if you are being laughed at in your dream, you may feel that someone is mocking you.

Laundry

Your laundry represents the most intimate and personal aspects of yourself. If the laundry is dirty, then you may have a secret or feel guilty about something you have done. Have you acted in a way that you believe to be immoral? Are you hiding a dirty little secret? Dreaming about washing your clothes indicates that it is time to come clean.

Leaf

A tree represents the life cycle and the leaves represent your position within the life cycle. For example, budding leaves suggest vitality and a new beginning, whereas falling leaves suggest the end of a cycle.

Consider whether these interpretations are adequate descriptions of your life now.

Leak

Leaks represent depleting resources. In dreams, leaks are typically water leaks and therefore suggest draining emotions. Consider who or what may be robbing you of your most valuable emotions, such as time and energy, then take steps to eliminate those negative influences in your life. Leaks may also suggest an aspect of your personal life that is no longer private.

Leg

Your legs ground and propel you through this world and in your dreams may prove to serve or deter you. Consider the stability of your legs in your dreams as they indicate the stability of your confidence. If your legs are wobbling, you may feel uncertainty regarding your life's course. A broken leg suggests a setback in achieving your goals.

Letter

When you receive a letter in your dream, consider it a gift; a message from yourself to yourself. As you progress in your dream work you may find yourself receiving letters in your dream and will be able to recall fragments of the content of each letter. Pay careful attention to the letter's words as they will reveal your soul's deepest desires. Until then, you should feel comforted knowing that the receipt of a letter in your dreams suggests a positive step along the path of self-awareness.

Library

A library represents the vast body of knowledge you contain about yourself and the universe, based on your life experiences and the experiences of humankind, but that is often unexplored. Consider the category of books you are perusing as they suggest various internal resources that you may need to reach within yourself. For example, old books represent wisdom and encyclopedias represent factual information.

Light

Light represents your ability to understand something that was previously inperceptible. The quality and strength of the light often mirrors your confidence in your knowledge. For example, the lighting of a match represents a fleeting moment of awareness whereas a bright light shining from heaven might imply enlightenment.

Lighthouse

Dreaming about a lighthouse implies that you are searching for guidance and protection during your journey toward self-awareness. Perhaps you have reached a point in your journey that has caused you to question your core beliefs. Don't be discouraged. The fact that you dreamed about the lighthouse is an indication that if you continue your journey you will find guidance.

Lightning

Lightning is a powerful phenomenon that is at once creative and destructive and suggests a sudden change in thinking. What activity were you engaged in when the lightning struck in your dream? For example, if you were swimming in your dream, which suggests exploring your emotions, you may have recently experienced an emotional upheaval.

Lion

A lion represents courage and leadership. Dreaming about being attacked by a lion suggests that you do not believe in your ability to stand up to a dangerous situation. If you attack a lion, then you feel that your leadership is being threatened in your waking life.

Liquid

The progress of your emotions is represented by the flow of liquid in your dreams. You are capable of infinite adaptation and change and the flow of the liquid represents the current state of your emotions. Is the liquid flowing smoothly? Is there a barrier that is not allowing the liquid to flow properly?

Lizard

A lizard represents your basic needs and drives, such as the instinct to connect with others and fight for survival. Consider your own basic drives during this period in your life. If you are running from the lizard, you do not want to acknowledge your basic needs.

Lock

If you have a problem that you do not think can be solved, you may dream of a locked object, such as a door or box. Searching for a key to unlock the object or unsuccessfully trying different keys in the lock indicates that you are searching for answers. If you dream of holding or housing a locked object, you desire to keep something about yourself or your life protected.

Lost

Dreams about being lost indicate that you are going through a period of transition or uncertainty and you do not know what course to take in life. This type of dream is an indication of extreme anxiety.

Searching for a lost object indicates an aspect of yourself that you fear you may be losing as represented in the lost object. For example, if you dream of losing your purse, which represents your identity, then you fear losing your individuality in a relationship.

Lottery

In waking life, winning the lottery represents the achievement of life-time financial security and dreaming about the lottery is an indication that you are concerned about your future financial success. If you hold a ticket in your dream, you are acknowledging the role chance plays in the attainment of wealth. You may be working long hours and are uncertain whether or not your hard work will pay off. Do not exhaust yourself. This dream is a good indication that your work is done and when your hard work meets opportunity, you will find financial success.

Machine

Dreams about machinery highlight your attitude about a world without emotion or compassion. You may have entered a time in your life when you feel that your social routines, such as work, or role as a parent or partner, are robbing you of passion and creativity. The dream may also reflect a larger social concern about the industrialization of our culture.

Magic

If you dream about magic, you are being alerted to your capacity to create false assumptions or illusions. Have you been trying to deceive yourself or others? Have you recently told a white lie? Are you maintaining a front so that others won't see your true emotions or intentions? Most people recognize the deceptiveness of magic and your dream is an indication that those you are trying to deceive recognize the illusion.

Make-Up

Applying cosmetics in your dream or noticing that you are wearing a lot of make-up in your dream suggests a subconscious desire to improve your image by falsifying it. Have you been hiding something from those you care about? The dream suggests that you are afraid people won't accept you for who you are so you change your image to suit the situation. Give people the benefit of the doubt.

Man

All men in your dreams represent an aspect of yourself whether you are a man or a woman. During your dream an aspect of yourself will be revealed to you through this person. What are his primary characteristics? For example, a man may represent typically masculine traits such as authority, dominance, or sexual energy, or the male figure in your dream may carry specific connections for you. Consider the predominant traits of the man and ask yourself how they relate to your own life and current situation.

Mansion

If a house represents the different aspects or activities in your life, then a mansion and its rooms exaggerate those aspects of yourself. For example, a kitchen represents the need for emotional nourishment and support. A kitchen in a mansion represents the nourishment as well, but suggests a much greater need.

Manure

Manure symbolizes the unwholesome or animalistic aspects of your personality that you consider worthless and no longer useful. If you are walking through manure, you feel consumed by your animalistic nature and unable to alter your behavior. Shoveling manure suggests a desire to remove these qualities from your life.

Map

A map represents your life's plan and the direction you want to go in life. It suggests that you need a guide and cannot always exist on intuition alone. Not being able to read a map indicates confusion about your life's path and not having a map indicates a loss of direction. The guidance you need comes from within and by paying attention to your dreams and practicing patience you will uncover the direction and purpose of your life.

Mask

A mask suggests a desire to take on another identity. Consider the type of mask you are wearing as it indicates the identity you would like to assume. For example, wearing an animal mask suggests that you are portraying the attributes of that animal to the outside world. Are you not allowing people to see you for who you really are?

Mattress

A mattress represents the private, personal aspects of your life. If the mattress is too big for a room, your dream is alerting you to the fact that sex plays too large a role in your life. If you dream of a mattress without a mattress pad or sheets, then you are likely exposing aspects of your personal life that should be kept private.

Maze

Dreams about mazes indicate that you are feeling uncertain about an aspect of your life or life in general. The good news about maze dreams is that they indicate a desire to find your way through this difficult period despite potential barriers. Maze dreams also serve to remind you that you must rely on intuition as well as logic to discover your life's purpose.

Medal

A medal highlights your feelings regarding a recent accomplishment. Receiving a medal indicates that you believe a job has been well done, whereas withholding a medal indicates that you believe adequate recognition has not been received.

Medicine

Dreams involving medicine suggest that you are in need of physical or mental healing. Have you been avoiding visiting your doctor about a health concern? Are you facing a personal crisis and do you need to confide in a trusted friend or therapist? This dream is acknowledging that the help you need may have to come from an external source.

Mermaid

A mermaid is a feminine symbol that represents the duality of the human spirit. The mermaid's tail represents the subconscious and the body represents the conscious. Most fables involving mermaids revolve around her desire to transform. Dreaming about a mermaid is a reminder that in order to live fully you must learn to integrate both aspects in your life.

Microscope

If you dream of looking through a microscope, this is an indication that you need to objectively scrutinize a particular aspect of your life. Rather than looking at a particular problem as a whole, you may need to pick apart the pieces and examine them one by one. The item that is being examined may also provide clues as to the area of your life that needs to be examined more carefully.

Milk

Milk represents your desire to be nurtured or to nurture. If you are in a relationship in which you feel more like someone's mother than their lover, you may dream about pouring that person a glass of milk. Spilled milk suggests that your need to nurture or desire to be nurtured has gotten out of hand.

Mirror

Looking in a mirror represents how you see yourself objectively and signifies a current stage of self-awareness. This new found self-awareness is related to vanity or at least self-image. If the reflection in the mirror is not your own, the person in the mirror may represent a part of yourself that you do not normally see that needs to be integrated into your own personality. If you view your reflection in a body of water, you are examining your subconscious.

Miscarriage

Birth represents the beginning of a new project; therefore, a miscarriage represents the abrupt and unwanted end to a new project. Has a project either at home or at work ended before it even had a chance to get off the ground? Is the termination of the project causing you to feel guilt or pain? You may want to consider resurrecting the project after a short hiatus.

Money

Money represents your attitude toward the material world. If the money is causing stress or anxiety in your dream world, then you are likely experiencing similar emotions in your waking life. What you are purchasing with the money is a good indication of those things you value in life. Money may also represent your personal resources, financial or emotional, and your ability to successfully handle those resources.

Monkey

Monkeys represent your mischievous, playful and impulsive side. This dream may be compensatory if you have been too serious or pragmatic in your waking life. If the monkeys in your dream are causing damage or destruction due to their mischievous behavior, the dream may be a warning that you are not taking life seriously enough.

Monster

When fears are blown out of proportion in your waking life, they may reveal themselves as monsters in your dreams. Now that you are an adult, you know better than to assume that monsters live under the bed or in the closet, so instead they appear in your dreams. You may be afraid of failure, a physical catastrophe, or a past trauma. Confronting your fears is the most effective way to eliminate them.

Moon

The gravitational forces between the earth and moon cause the tides to rise and fall and in dreams the moon represents the natural, cyclical knowledge of our subconscious. Your enlightenment will not happen overnight, it is only through learning to observe and intuit your subconscious emotions that you can begin the journey toward enlightenment.

Mother

The feminine characteristics inherent in your relationships are often reflected in dreams about your mother. This is less a dream about you and more a dream about how you relate to other people. Your mother's primary traits, or those she exhibits in your dream, are indicators of the attributes that you need to more carefully examine in your current relationships. In general, dreams involving your mother relate to the feminine qualities in your relationships, such as your ability to create life and nurture.

Motorcycle

Motorcycles are generally considered symbol of freedom, independence, and risk-taking. If you are riding a motorcycle in your dream, then you are exhibiting these qualities on your life's journey. If you are the passenger on a motorcycle, you may be riding on someone else's coattails and their independence and risk-taking are propelling you forward. Ask yourself whether or not you find these qualities admirable. If so, it may be time to start taking your own risks.

Mountain

A mountain symbolizes a personal goal or challenge that you must face. A mountain represents a greater challenge than a smaller body of land, such as a hill. Your ability to climb the mountain indicates your attitude toward the task ahead of you. If you dream of standing on top of a mountain, you are subconsciously aware of overcoming an important obstacle or of gaining perspective.

Mouse

A mouse represents those personal traits that you believe are often unnoticed or insignificant. What qualities do you feel that others are overlooking? Devise a plan to get people to take notice. You may also dream about mice if you are a timid or shy person. Your reaction to the mice in your dreams may indicate your attitude about these characteristics within yourself
.

Mouth

Mouths represent your ability to communicate. Dreams that focus on the mouth are indicative of the role communication plays in your life. For example, if you are unable to speak or your mouth is sealed shut, you may be having difficulty expressing yourself.

Movie

You're watching a horror movie and the femme fatale is running back into the house after Freddie or Jason chases her through the yard. You're thinking, "Are you crazy? Don't go in there!" It's amazing how easily we can criticize the decisions stars make on screen. Dreaming about the movies provides you with the unique opportunity to observe the roles you play in your life and objectively review your actions and experiences, good or bad. The actors represent various aspects of your personality and the action represents the activities in your life.

Mud

Water represents the conscious mind and the earth represents the subconscious. Therefore, dreaming about mud is pointing to the fact that you need to work on combining these two sides of yourself.

Murder

Who is being murdered? This person being killed represents an aspect of you that you actively want to change or destroy. For example, if you believe that the person being killed is arrogant and greedy, then these are the qualities you wish to eliminate in yourself. If you are the murderer in your dreams, then you are acknowledging that you have the necessary resources to change your behavior.

Museum

Museums highlight the aspects of your past that you most treasure. If you dream of an art museum, for example, you are paying tribute to your past creative accomplishments. A history museum points to a past life experience that you may need to acknowledge or reexamine.

Music

Music provides clues about the feeling or mood of the dream. The feeling associated with the dream will depend on your personal feelings about the type of music. For example, you may find heavy metal music energizing, whereas someone else may think it is distracting or anxiety producing.

Nail

Nails represent your potential to build relationships. If you dream of nails, you are likely building or tearing down an object. Building an object, such as a piece of furniture or house, indicates a desire to develop a relationship, whereas tearing nails out of an object suggests a desire to destroy a relationship.

Naked

The real you stripped of all pretense appears as your naked self in your dream world. Perhaps you feel that you are being exposed in your waking life. If the dream is anxiety provoking, such as dreaming of being naked in public, you may fear that you are vulnerable to the opinion of others. If your nakedness is alluring, you are comfortable with who you are.

Needle

A sewing or knitting needle represents your desire to mend or repair. Is there a relationship in need of repair? Consider the item you are creating as this may further suggest the area in your life in need of repair. For example, mending a dress indicates a desire to restore your femininity.

Nest

A nest represents your home and its condition, and the action surrounding the nest suggests your feelings about the safety of your home life. If someone is knocking a nest out of a tree, for example, you may feel that your home life is in jeopardy. If you dream about a bird tending to its nest, you may wish to spend more time at home taking care of domestic chores.

Newspaper

Newspapers represent information and your perceptions regarding the world. Note the section of the paper you are reading as it will point to your concerns. If you are reading the business pages, you may have anxiety about your financial resources. Reading the help wanted ads suggest fear about losing your job.

Nose

The nose represents curiosity or intuition. Is your nose larger than normal in your dream? Perhaps you are sticking your nose in where it does not belong. Are you sniffing out the truth? You may be suspicious about someone or something in your waking life and that is being pointed out in your dream.

Number

When people dream about numbers, they are inclined to spend time finding precognitive meaning in the dream, such as winning lottery numbers, number of children they will have or years they will be married. More than likely, however, dreams about numbers point to your past and connect to important dates in your life, such as year of birth or house number.

Nun

A nun represents virtue and wholesomeness, qualities that you likely suspect you need more of in your life. Because nuns practice abstinence, the dream may further indicate that you are too promiscuous. Perhaps a brief period of celibacy is in order to help you refocus your priorities.

Nurse

Your attitudes toward healing are reflected in dreams containing nurses. Dreaming about a mean or unsympathetic nurse may indicate a fear of finding out information about your health, whereas a kind nurse indicates a desire to be nurtured. Ask yourself if you have any reason to be concerned about your health and make an appointment, if necessary.

Ocean

Water represents your conscious life experiences, particularly emotions. The ocean as a water symbol, due to its vastness, further suggests the collective conscious. The action related to the ocean, such as sailing, diving, or swimming, provides additional clues to the dream's meaning, as will the condition of the water.

Office

Your office is a place of productivity and professional responsibility and dreams about this location indicate your attitude toward your professional life. Examine the office's condition and the objects in it to determine the significance of this dream. For example, a messy office may indicate chaos in your professional life and an office that is nearly empty may suggest that you feel you are being underutilized.

Opera

Dreaming of an opera allows you to objectively view your life and its key events. Unlike a play, an opera is an exaggeration of the people and events in your life. The opera singer is an exaggeration of you. Consider why your subconscious allows you to view your life as an opera rather than as a play or a movie. It may be because you are over-dramatizing your situation.

Orange

Orange symbolizes sexual energy as it relates to fertility and reproduction. If you dream about orange objects, consider the subtly sexual aspects of that object's meaning. For example, a vase represents beauty and growth in your relationship. Therefore, an orange vase suggests beauty and growth as it relates to fertility. In this case, you may be ready to begin a family.

Orchestra

An orchestra is a basic example of different people working together toward a common goal and achieving a harmonious effect. Dreaming of an orchestra suggests that you are trying to achieve harmony in life by bringing together the various and seemingly different aspects of self, such as mind, body and spirit.

Orgy

Dreaming about an orgy indicates an excess of sexual energy and a desire to overindulge. If you are watching, but not participating in the sexual acts, you may feel like you are not in control of your sexuality. Reclaim your sexuality by acknowledging your desires and finding healthy outlets for them.

Orphan

If an event in your life has recently resurrected subconscious childhood fears of abandonment, you may dream of an orphan. If you believe you are the orphan in your dream, you are feeling unloved in your waking life and fear that you will be left alone. This is an indication to build your confidence and resist overdependence on another person. If you are helping or observing an orphan, you may feel that someone in your life needs to be nurtured or rescued.

Oven

Dreaming about an oven is a sign of encouragement from your subconscious indicating that you have the ability to transform and create. Perhaps you are on the brink of a new project and the ideas are beginning to incubate and take shape. You should continue to forge ahead with your plans even if the process has been difficult.

Owl

Owls represent intuition and wisdom and their appearance in dreams should be considered an important message from the subconscious. Owls often appear in dreams as messengers to alert you to the importance of your dream. They also appear in your dream right before its main point, so pay careful attention to the events that follow an owl's appearance.

Package

A package represents an aspect of you that you are either giving or receiving. If you are sending the package, this indicates that you are letting go of a certain aspect of yourself. Similarly, receiving a package indicates embracing a particular aspect of your personality. Consider the presentation of the package as this will provide further information about the value you place on what you are giving or receiving. For example, if the package is an elegantly wrapped gift, then the quality you are sharing is one that is of high value to you.

Painting

Painting as a verb suggests concealing an experience or attitude. Viewing a painting is suggestive of your attitude toward creativity and creating a piece of art is related to feelings about self-expression. Detailed paintings indicate that you must focus in on the details of life, whereas a large canvas suggests adopting a broad overview. The subject and colors in the painting may provide further clues about the dream's meaning.

Pants

Pants represent sexuality and authority. If you are wearing the pants in your dream, then you feel confident and in control of the dream theme. Losing your pants suggests a loss of control, and dirty pants represent authority that is based on impure actions or thoughts.

Paper

Papers communicate ideas that are of importance to you, so it is important to notice the type of document in the dream. For example, a contract may indicate an agreement that needs to be reached in your life, a bank statement might indicate your financial resources, and blank paper indicates the need to express something.

Parachute

A parachute represents your ability to overcome fears. It is a signal to trust that the skills you have developed will protect you from life's obstacles. On the other hand, if you dream that your parachute will not open you feel anxious about being prepared to handle life's difficulties. Consider how you can prepare yourself to handle difficulties in your waking life before disaster strikes.

Paralysis

At some point in our lives, we've all felt emotionally paralyzed by fear or guilt. If you are feeling guilty or afraid, you may dream about physical paralysis. Paralysis dreams can be frightening as they conjure our worst fears about our ability to move through life; they suggest lack of will and control. Attend to your soul's desires and acknowledge and address the fears in your waking life to put an end to paralyzing dreams.

Party

Dreams that involve parties relate to your social life. Dream parties may provide you with an opportunity to objectively view and hone your social skills. If you are the host of the party, the dream is an examination of the different aspects of yourself as represented by your guests. If you are the guest of honor at the party, you have a desire for love or attention.

Passport

Passports indicate identity beyond your domestic roles. For example, in addition to being a wife and mother, you may also identify yourself as an artist or doctor. Also, dreaming about a passport indicates a desire to gain exposure to influences outside of your immediate circle. Is there an exotic location that you have longed to explore, but have you put off travel plans due to personal or professional obligations? This dream may be an indication that it's time to call your travel agent.

Path

On your life's journey there are many different paths or approaches you may choose and dreams about paths point to the many options available to you. Practice the art of lucid dreaming, the ability to control the actions in your dreams due to the knowledge that you are dreaming, and select different paths to take each time you have this dream. This will allow you to explore your various life paths and the consequences associated with them.

Pen/Pencil

Your ability to communicate is represented in a pen or a pencil. Unlike verbal communication, however, the written word provides a more accurate and lasting account of your thoughts. Because of its permanence, a pen suggests a more confident attitude toward the ideas you are communicating. A pen that runs out of ink indicates that you are unable to communicate based on current knowledge. Sharpening pencils indicates preparation for an important event.

Penis

The penis represents fertility, power, and sexual drive and suggests your attitude toward these aspects of self. A shriveled or small penis suggests feeling a loss of power, for example.

People

All people in your dreams represent an aspect of yourself. When trying to determine the meaning of a dream, consider the major characteristics of each person and determine what about that characteristic or attribute relates to you. See separate listings for adolescent, baby, child, fireman, judge, magician, policeman, king, soldier, stranger, and teacher.

Perspire

Perspiration suggests intense emotion or discomfort. You may dream about perspiring when a situation in your dream is emotionally or physically difficult. You may not be consciously aware that this particular experience makes you uncomfortable, but your subconscious does. Consider the event in question and develop strategies in your life to cope with uncomfortable situations.

Photograph

Photographs represent memories or experiences from your past. For example, if you dream about a photograph of you and your father from when you were a child, you may have an unresolved childhood issue with your father or it may be a reminder of an error you made in that relationship. Similarly, a photo of you will suggest an aspect of your life in need of careful consideration. Consider the photograph an indication to resolve an old issue or to not make the same mistake again in a current relationship or other area of your life.

Piano

A piano represents your creative potential and ability to express that creativity. The piano is also a sensual and graceful instrument that further suggests that subtle changes or nuances in behavior can affect your creativity. Have you recently felt creatively blocked? How skilled are you in self-expression? Are you stumbling through your exercises, or hitting each key with precision?

Pig

Pigs represent gluttony and slovenliness along with other distasteful qualities. Either you or someone in your life is exhibiting qualities that you believe to be "piggish" in nature. Consider what aspect of your life this relates to and confront it head-on.

Pillow

Pillows provide comfort and support and their appearance in dreams indicates your need for both. If you are going through a difficult period, a pillow may be a reminder to look to others for support. It may also be an indication to rely less on others and more on your own abilities. Because pillows are associated with sleep and relaxation, lack of support in your life may be causing you tension or may be interfering with your ability to rest and relax.

Planet

The planets represent the universal nature of humankind. In this cosmic collective conscious, the earth represents self, the sun represents the soul, and the planets represent different world views, such as:

Mercury, intuition and communication; Venus, love; Mars, aggression; Jupiter, growth; Saturn, fate; Uranus, change; Neptune, the conscious; Pluto, the subconscious. You may have difficulty identifying the planets in your dreams beyond the earth, sun, and moon at first, but in time their appearance in your dreams will help you identify what ways of thinking are influencing your life.

Plant

Plants represent personal growth and the type of plant in your dream will help you discover the area of your life undergoing development. For example, weeds represent the negative mental thoughts and attitudes that encroach on our happiness, whereas the rose represents your romantic relationships. Pay attention to how you are cultivating the plants in your dreams to help you assess your current level of development.

Plate

Plates represent your daily domestic routines and activities and their decorativeness or lack of design suggests your level of satisfaction with your domestic roles. In addition, a full plate indicates that you have an abundance of responsibilities and challenges and an empty plate suggests that your domestic life is not full or complete. Spend some time examining your daily activities as dreaming of plates is an indication that you need to reexamine your priorities.

Pocket

Pockets contain those items that you want to protect. In your waking life, these might be your wallet and personal identification, but in your dream those items may represent your secrets or memories. If a pickpocket is harassing you, you may fear disclosure; and if items are missing from your pockets, you may believe that old memories are fading. Has a recent situation caused memories or secrets to wreak havoc on your personal life?

Police Officer

Police officers represent social morals and authority. A police pursuit, with you as the main suspect, suggests that you feel guilty about something you have said or done. Ask yourself if there is something you are trying to escape from or avoid in your waking life. If a police officer appears as one of many characters in the background of your dream, you may be seeking protection in your waking life. Is there someone or something that you fear?

Pool

Swimming pools represent specific conscious life experiences, such as a single event or life experience. Diving into a pool means that you need to delve more deeply into the emotions surrounding the event. Diving into a pool with no water suggests that you are unprepared to examine the event and may need additional time or experience to delve into that topic. Once you have determined the experience that the dream is related to, consider whether you are giving that experience adequate attention in your waking life.

Pregnancy

If you are trying to conceive or are pregnant, dreaming about being pregnant allows you to explore your feelings and confront your anxieties about this important life decision. If you are not dealing with pregnancy issues, dreaming of being pregnant suggests the incubation of an idea or the beginning of a new project. What ideas have been germinating in your waking life? Your subconscious may be indicating the idea's potential.

Prison

Being imprisoned in your dreams suggests feelings of isolation and confinement in your waking life. Prisons further suggest self-imposed loneliness due to actions you believe to be immoral. Escaping from prison indicates that you are ready to let go of out-dated or negative attitudes. Often you are your own worst judge and jury. Outdated or negative thoughts and beliefs, such as guilt, fear or ignorance can leave you feeling imprisoned.

Prostitute

Sex dreams are rarely about sex and dreaming about a prostitute has little to do with promiscuity. If you dream about a prostitute, you are being alerted to your degraded morals. For example, you may feel that you have sold yourself out in your professional or personal life. The only way to regain your self-respect is to right your wrong.

Puppet

Dreaming about a puppet suggests that you are feeling manipulated or desire to manipulate someone else. Perhaps you are feeling a loss of control in your personal or professional life. This dream is an indication that you are feeling powerless.

Purple

The color purple connotes royalty and spiritual transformation. Dreaming about purple may indicate that you feel you have fallen from grace, so you surround yourself with purple objects that represent royalty in your dreams. Your dream may also be an indication that you have achieved the next level of growth in your spiritual transformation.

Purse

A purse is where you keep your most personal possessions, particularly your identification. Women often dream of losing or not being able to find their purse. If you have this dream, it is an indication that you are anxious about losing your identity. Perhaps you are embracing beliefs that are not your own. Stop letting your relationships and life experiences rob you of your identity.

Pyramid

The Egyptians built pyramids to their Gods in the hope of becoming immortal. This spiritual symbol indicates that the dream is about your feelings about death and the mysteries of the afterlife. Your level of awareness and acceptance about death will be indicated in the action related to the pyramid. It may be time to become more aware of your own spirituality and to seek answers in ancient readings.

Queen

It would be good to be the queen, wouldn't it? Dreaming about a queen indicates your desire to control or rule your environment. In what area of your life do you feel like you have lost control? Do you have the desire to have others serve you? Your dream is an indication that you are aware of the power you have to regain control of your life.

Quicksand

Quicksand represents a loss of control and feelings of helplessness. If you are feeling insecure in your waking life, this fear may manifest in your dreams. Dreams involving quicksand further suggest that the problem you are confronting was unforeseen and may have little to do with your own actions. Nonetheless, this problem needs to be resolved, even if the conflict has little to do with you personally, as it is still causing you pain.

Quilt

A quilt represents various aspects of our familial past that provide comfort. Perhaps it is the knowledge that you have good genes, the tendency toward long life, or inherited good looks. Attempt to identify the quilt as you may have seen it before, but its memory is buried. If it is your grandmother or mother's quilt, for example, you may be in need of nurturing from a woman in your life. This dream is a reminder to ask for the support you need from those closest to you.

Rabbit

A rabbit represents rapid movement through life. Do you feel that your life is moving too fast? Despite a rabbit's swiftness, it is also known for its overconfidence. Its appearance in your dream may be a reminder to plan ahead and slow down. Rabbits also suggest fertility and reproductive health. If you have been having difficulty conceiving, you may dream of a rabbit. Again, this dream is a reminder to pace yourself.

Race

A race indicates your competitiveness in life and your desire to get ahead. Are you falling behind or struggling to complete the race? If so, you may feel that you are not participating actively in life and that your current resources are not sufficient to help you succeed. Find out what drives your competitiveness and consider alternatives to reaching your goal.

Radio

Ideas and beliefs that are not your own are often heard through a radio in your dreams. You should assume that any information received from a radio in your dreams is suspicious and does not reflect your personal beliefs. Are you allowing other people to influence your actions? This dream is a reminder not to believe everything you hear. In order to break away from the pack mentality, you should only listen to your own inner voice.

Raft

A raft represents the beliefs you know would not hold up if put to the test. It may also represent a temporary period or situation in your life. A raft can get you through a rough period, but its appearance in your dreams signifies that you need to build a more solid foundation of beliefs in order to make it through a prolonged, difficult period.

Railway

A railway represents your life's journey as it relates to your professional experiences or group organizations. A railway suggests the enormous energy and power within a particular group or organization that is difficult to change. You have created a powerful impact on a particular group or organization and its force is unstoppable. Now all you can do is sit back and see what happens.

Rain

Rain represents the emotions that make up your conscious life experiences and the type of rain indicate the nature of the emotions. For example, a storm suggests a difficult time in your life, light rain represents cleansing, and hail represents painful emotions. The time of day that the rain occurs may provide additional clues about the emotions the rain represents. For example, evening rain suggests depression, whereas morning rain represents potential.

Rainbow

Hope is epitomized in the image of the rainbow. You may be going through a difficult period in your life and the rainbow is a reminder that magic and beauty are often the result of difficult emotions. The rainbow is a reminder to dream big dreams but to also remain grounded.

Raincoat

Your desire to protect yourself from outside influences is represented in a raincoat. Wearing a raincoat may be related to fear of criticism. If you fear judgment, you may be conducting an aspect of your life in such a manner that makes you feel guilty. Be proactive. Ask friends and family for constructive criticism, then try to engage yourself in a dream for possible alternative strategies to the situation that you can't think of consciously.

Rape

As with most sex dreams, rape dreams are rarely about sex. Instead, they suggest that you feel violated or victimized in an area of your life. This nightmare suggests a loss of control and is a warning to consider areas of life where you may be allowing others to control you. Think about the primary characteristics of the attacker in order to determine where in your life you feel you may be losing control, then review your response to the rape. Were you fighting your attacker, for example? If so, you recognize your own power.

Rat

The rat represents what you believe to be your negative qualities, particularly deceit. Have you recently committed a despicable act toward a friend, family member or coworker? If you have recently told a lie or acted in a similarly deceitful manner, you may dream of a rat. Recognizing both the positive and negative aspects of your personality is the first step toward correcting your behavior.

Reading

Dreaming about reading is an indication that you are committed to looking inward and are actively seeking knowledge. This dream is a realization that the knowledge you are seeking exists within yourself in your memory and experiences. Your subconscious is asking you to turn away from external influences in your quest for self-knowledge because the only real answers are found within yourself.

Red

Red symbolizes intense emotions. For example, dreaming about receiving red flowers suggests a desire for passion and love, whereas a deserted red barn may represent your habitual anger.

Refrigerator

If you have recently received a new form of nourishment, such as knowledge or love, your desire to preserve or protect this new acquisition may appear as a refrigerator in your dreams. For example, if the refrigerator is not running properly, you may fear that your knowledge or love will quickly spoil. It is impossible for you to protect yourself from losing those things you love the most, so acknowledge the fear but do not dwell on this image.

Rescue

When you are not feeling strong enough to stand on your own physically or emotionally, you may dream of being rescued. This dream symbol is an indication that you have an overreliance on others. You need to learn to stand on your own two feet or you will always be indebted to others.

Restaurant

A restaurant represents a desire to receive emotional nourishment from external sources. For example, dreaming of an enjoyable dinner with friends indicates that you are not satisfying your needs as a social creature. Call a friend to see a movie or host a dinner party ASAP!

Ring

All circles represent wholeness, but rings are unique in that they also imply unity in relationships. A gift of a ring is considered a sign of commitment and receiving a ring in your dream suggests your desire to make a commitment in your current relationship. A ring on your right hand suggests that the dream is about your feelings about marriage in general or your current spouse in particular. If the ring is worn on the left hand, your dream may be about your dissatisfaction in your current relationship. If you are married, you may have a subconscious desire to divorce.

River

A river symbolizes the direction and movement of your conscious emotions. Is the river flooding? If so, you may feel inundated with emotion and may need to speak with a friend. A stagnant river may indicate a dullness or lack of emotion, in which case you need to identify why your emotional well has run dry. Crossing a river represents making a change or taking a chance. If you are standing in the river, you are feeling engulfed by your emotions. Swimming upstream means that you are resisting your feelings—most likely your intuitive desires.

Road

Examine the destination and condition of the road in your dream to uncover your approach to life. A winding road suggests your tendency to become distracted, whereas a straight road indicates a clear goal. A cul-de-sac or dead-end suggests helplessness. The condition of the road and its ease of travel is an indication of your difficulty or success on your life journey.

Rock

A rock represents strength of character and is an indication that your reliability is in question. In your waking life, are others relying on you more often than usual or are you leaning on others for support? You have not developed a solid foundation for your soul and should spend time cultivating your core values.

Rocket

A rocket is a positive dream symbol reminding you of your own energy and ability to reach unimaginable heights. Do you have a lofty dream that has been on the back burner due to work or family commitments? It is time to tap into every last energy reserve you have to attain that goal.

Roof

A roof is a barrier between your emotional life and your spiritual life, and its appearance in your dreams suggests the strategies you are using to tap into your spiritual side. For example, standing on a roof means that you have achieved enlightenment, a leaky roof means that there are faults in your thinking, and mending a roof means that you are exploring new avenues to develop awareness.

Rope

A rope highlights feelings of restraint. If you are being bound with rope, you may feel that someone is trying to control you. If someone is tying your hands, then they are trying to keep you from acting. Is someone trying to control you or restrain your freedom? A rope may also indicate a desire to be rescued if someone throws it to you in your dream.

Running

This dream symbol can be interpreted literally to mean that you are running away from something in your waking life. Is there a situation or person that you are trying to avoid? Have you been procrastinating about beginning an unpleasant task? You are likely hoping to avoid potentially painful emotions by running away from them. In order to resolve your problems, you must confront them head-on.

Sailing

Sailing dreams highlight how you navigate through your emotions. If you are skilled and the waters are calm, you are entering an emotionally satisfying period. If, on the other hand, you are having difficulty with the sails and the water is rough, you are in an emotionally unstable period in your life. The boat's sails are a reminder that natural forces can carry you through emotionally difficult periods. However, the boat cannot be propelled by force alone, it needs a confident and skilled guide. A sailor represents freedom and confidence in navigating emotions.

Sand

Sand represents the breakdown of your core values. Although you may feel that your character is strong, dreaming of sand is a warning that your core values are being put to the test. Would you be able to write down the four core values that define who you are if asked? Sometimes the simple act of identifying and documenting your values will protect them from outside influences.

Saw

The gradual breakdown of your long-standing opinions and beliefs is represented in dreams about sawing. Has an event recently occurred that has caused you to question things you once believed to be true? This event will not have been a sudden or startling event, but something that has happened slowly and without notice. Once you have identified the event, try to determine who or what caused you to question your beliefs related to the event.

School

Dreams about school, particularly high school, indicate your feelings about your social skills. If you are the student, are you cutting class, wandering the halls, or actively participating in class discussion? This is an indication of your self-acceptance regarding your social roles. Are you taking on a new challenge or learning a new skill in your waking life that is forcing you to explore your role in social situations? Have you started a new job and feel like you are learning the rules of the game all over again? Are you feeling left out of events that are important to you? School dreams often involve anxiety-provoking situations, such as taking an exam, not being able to find your classroom, or realizing halfway through a semester that you haven't been attending one of your classes. When school dreams involve anxiety, it indicates that you are feeling vulnerable about a current social situation.

Scissors

Scissors indicate your desire to sever a relationship. If the scissors are blunt, you may wish to end a relationship, but are having difficulty cutting ties. Scissors further suggest decisiveness and the fact that you are dreaming about them indicates that you are ready to let go. You may have been uncertain about someone or something in your life that you believe to be negative or nonessential up to this point.

Searching

You are not alone in your search for love, happiness, and truth. What current problem is in need of answering? If the dream is anxiety-provoking, this is an indication that you are anxious to uncover the purpose of your life. Your dream is attempting to teach you that the process of searching is just as important as what you find. You will spend most of your life searching for answers and the best approach toward this search is one of excited exploration.

Seasons

The seasons represent the phases of your life. The specific season will indicate your attitude regarding the period of life you are in at this moment. Consider whether the season is representative of the actual phase of your life now. If not, you may have anxiety about an upcoming stage or are still harboring resentments about the past. See separate listings for winter, spring, summer, and fall.

Seed

In every seed lies the potential for growth and life. You may be on the brink of a new project or new phase of life and this is represented in dreams about seeds. Perhaps you are planting a garden, in which case you are laying the necessary foundation to achieve growth. The seed also connotes images of the sperm and eating a seed may suggest your desire to become pregnant.

Sewing

The desire to mend a relationship is often represented in dreams about sewing. Hand sewing represents a relationship from your past and machine sewing represents a current relationship. Consider whom you may need to connect with in your waking life. Changing your outlook or attitude may be all that is needed to repair the relationship or create a new one.

Sex

Surprisingly, sex dreams are not usually about sex. They are about the attitudes and characteristics that you believe are underdeveloped. Consider the major characteristic of the person with whom you are having sex, then ask yourself how that characteristic relates to this period in your life. For example, having sex with your boss suggests your need to maintain or embrace authority and sex with a celebrity indicates a desire to receive recognition. If you dream about having sex with your current crush, consider your attitude about the tryst. This is your subconscious' attempt to play out this possible scenario and the outcomes that may accompany it.

Shadow

Shadows represent the dark side of your personality. You, like everyone else, have dark aspects of your personality that you keep hidden and these alter egos are often represented as shadows or as shadowy figures. If you carry shame about the darker aspects of your personality, you may regularly dream about shadows. Being pursued by a shadowy figure indicates that you are afraid of your dark side. The easiest way to stop these dreams is to acknowledge and take responsibility for all aspects of your personality, good or bad.

Shampoo

Shampooing your hair highlights negative or useless thoughts that need to be removed from your life. Are you exhibiting sexist or racist behavior, for example? Are you indulging in self-pity, jealousy, or resentment? What has been weighing you down lately? This dream is an indication that it is time to clear your mind. If you find yourself shampooing someone else's hair, then you would like to change that person's negative attitude or beliefs.

Shaving

Dreams about shaving indicate your desire to reveal yourself to others. For example, shaving your head means that you want others to acknowledge your intellect and shaving your face indicates a desire for others to understand your inner feelings and attitudes. Is there an aspect of your personality that you are concealing that is making you uncomfortable?

Sheep

A sheep's most well known characteristic is its inclination to follow, and dreaming of sheep suggests that you are feeling manipulated. Have you been afraid to speak up at the office and break away from the pack? Are you always a follower, but rarely the leader? Are others influencing your decisions? This dream is an indication to abandon your herd mentality and break away from the pack.

Shell

Shells are associated with the ocean and, therefore, conscious life experiences, particularly emotions. Just as sea creatures utilize shells to protect them from their environment, so do humans. Dreaming about shells symbolizes your desire to withdraw from the outside world and seek protection. While spending time alone in quiet reflection can do a soul good, living like a hermit will not. Rejection and pain are a part of life that cannot be avoided.

Shirt

Shirts, particularly for men, represent the public self and as with most clothes the condition, color, and style provide further clues for interpretation. For example, a flashy shirt suggests that you think others see you as outgoing, and wearing an athletic shirt suggests that the dream is related to your physical or sexual abilities. Also consider that the dream may be an indication that you are paying too close attention to your outward appearances.

Shoe

Your confidence regarding the direction you are headed in life is represented in the type of shoes you wear in your dreams. For example, dirty old tennis shoes suggest that you feel unprepared for the journey ahead and your self esteem is low, hiking boots suggest a difficult road ahead, and slippers indicate a need to slow down and relax. Boost your image and your spiritual foundation by wearing well-maintained and stylish shoes in your waking life. Your subconscious self may take notice.

Shooting

To interpret a nocturnal shootout, it is necessary to remember who has been shot. While guns appear frequently in dreams, it is not often that you will actually witness yourself or someone else being shot. If this happens, someone has caused you severe emotional pain that has left you wounded. If you are the one who pulls the trigger, consider the characteristics of the individual who has been shot, as this represents an aspect of yourself that you wish to destroy. What aspects of your personality would you like to have eliminated?

Shopping

Your emotional needs are reflected in your nocturnal shopping sprees. Shopping for clothes highlights your need for acceptance and grocery shopping suggests a need for emotional nourishment, for example. You may find that you shop in your dreams for the same reason you shop in real life, to focus your energy on the external acquisition of objects rather than personal growth.

Shoulder

Atlas carried the weight of the world on his shoulders and you must too if you dream of this particular body part. Responsibility, duty, and honor can often become burdens and our subconscious may point this out when you are unable to acknowledge this in your waking life. Are you taking on too much responsibility at work? Do you feel responsible for an elderly parent?

Shovel

A shovel represents a desire to dig deeper into your subconscious and to uncover the mysteries of your soul. If you are having difficulty digging, you may be experiencing difficulties getting to the core of your subconscious desires. If you are easily utilizing the shovel, then you are feeling strong in your waking life. This dream is an indication that you need to explore the experiences or memories in your waking life that you dream about.

Shrinking

When you feel insignificant or powerless in a particular aspect of your life, you may dream of shrinking. If other people or objects appear diminutive, then those people or things have become less significant in your life. It is ironic that people or things that have become less significant in your life are important enough to be gleaned out of thousands of images in your waking life to appear in your dreams. Despite what you have led yourself to believe in your conscious or waking life, you may still feel threatened.

Sibling

Dreams about your siblings represent your competitive side. For example, if you dream about your older brother, who is more athletic than you are, the dream may be an indication that you are feeling out of shape or "off your game." If you dream about a younger brother, whom you always felt the need to protect, you may be willing to put aside your competitiveness to resolve a problem at home or at work.

Sickness

When you are sick, your body is out of harmony with its environment and sickness in dreams indicates that you are emotionally out of balance. Possibly you are infected by fear, guilt, anxiety, sadness or any other malady that infects humankind and can actually cause illness in waking life. Identify the emotion to which the dream points, then make a commitment to let go of this emotion in the future. Unexpressed emotions can lead to illness in your waking life.

Silver

Silver represents intuition, spirituality, and hope; its appearance in dreams is a positive omen.

Singing

Have you ever sung in the shower when you've been in a bad mood? Probably not—singing represents an inner contentment that can only come when you are happy and at peace with yourself and your environment. Pay attention to the words of the song to determine what is causing all this happiness, and then enjoy it.

Sinking

Dreaming of sinking suggests feelings of hopelessness. Sinking in a boat indicates that you are having difficulty handling the emotional aspects of life and sinking in sand indicates a loss of confidence related to the strength of our core values. As with every potential disaster, there is an opportunity for challenge and great heroism. Reflect on the aspect of your life that is causing you anxiety and think about how you might rise to meet the challenge.

Skin

The skin represents your ability to protect yourself. If you dream of a sunburn, you feel overexposed. Dry, itchy skin suggests raw or irritated emotions and oily skin or acne suggests that your problems are obvious to the outside world. Identify the areas of your life where you feel vulnerable in order to determine the meaning of this dream.

Skirt

If you notice that you are wearing a skirt in your dream, your subconscious is pointing out your feminine qualities as they relate to the dream environment. For example, a short skirt lends a sexually adventurous or promiscuous tone to the dream, whereas an ankle-length skirt suggests wholesomeness. Men and women share masculine and feminine traits. Don't be afraid to explore both.

Sky

The sky represents the potential of your mind and gazing at the sky suggests acknowledgment of that potential. If the sky is dark, you may doubt your potential, whereas a blue cloudless sky suggests confidence and feeling connected to the vastness of human potential. You must be on the brink of making a decision that could bring you closer to your intellectual or spiritual self.

Sleeping

It is unusual to dream about sleeping. Some believe that dreaming about sleep is the first step toward achieving an out of body experience. While you may never have an out of body experience, be assured that dreaming of sleep indicates heightened awareness. If others are in the room, watch their expressions and movements as these are indicators of their attitude toward your spiritual growth.

Smoke

Smoke suggests imminent danger or fear of danger. Because of smoke's connection to fire, the smoke may also indicate the potential for destruction. You should also consider the dual nature of fire. While it is destructive, it also leads to new beginnings and purification.

Snake

The snake represents your compulsive nature and habits. Your potential for good and evil may appear in your dream represented as a snake. Also, because of the snake's association with Adam and Eve, it represents temptation.

Snow

The interpretation of this symbol depends on your attitude toward snow and winter. For example, if you enjoy winter, snow may represent feelings of tranquility and purity. On the other hand, if you are a Palm Beach native recently relocated to Long Island, snow may represent hostile emotions.

Soldier

Soldiers and other members of the armed forces represent discipline, duty, and honor, and their appearance in your dream is an indication that you may need to more fully develop these qualities within yourself. Perhaps you have been lacking in self-discipline or have been shunning your responsibilities at home.

Speed

The force at which you progress through life is represented in rapidly moving objects, particularly cars. Speeding may suggest that your life is out of control or that you are too focused on the end result. Slow down. Sometimes the journey is more important than the destination.

Spider

A spider may appear in your dreams when there is something you feel anxious about, such as being caught in a lie or an act of deception. Consider the webs you have been weaving in your waking life in order to uncover the deeper meaning in your dream.

Spring

The seasons represents the phases of life and the spring is the most inspiring phase of all. It represents new life, new beginnings, and hope. Spring also represents your youth. If spring is the background for your dream, then you are likely engaged in a new project or relationship, or the dream is highlighting a particular aspect of your youth.

Squirrel

Those pesky rodents have an uncanny ability to scour the earth for anything that might be useful in the future. Dreaming of squirrels is an indication that you may need to examine your resources to ensure that you are prepared for the future.

Stage

The stage represents your life and the actors the various players in your life's drama. If you appear on stage, you may desire recognition. Viewing the stage from the perspective of an audience member provides you with an opportunity to view your life objectively.

Stealing

The verb "to steal" has powerful connotations and provokes feelings of injustice and anger in most individuals. Dreams about stealing have little to do with the actual object that is stolen. Consider what the object represents as that is likely what you believe someone has taken from you. For example, a guitar represents harmony, so if you dream that someone steals your guitar you may feel robbed of inner peace.

Stomach

Your ability to digest the events and circumstances of your life are represented in dreams that include the stomach as an image. If you are sick to your stomach, then you are unable to handle the difficult aspects of your life, and a nervous stomach indicates anxiety. A bare midriff is an indication that you are open and accepting to new experiences.

Stone

A stone represents family strength and solidarity. If you are pushing a large stone, such as a boulder, you may feel weighed down by a family relationship. It you are tossing or skipping stones, on the other hand, you are likely feeling freed by the protection your family relationships have to offer. Turning a stone over represents a desire to uncover the hidden aspects and different facets of your family's dynamics.

Storm

Storms indicate sudden and violent conflict in your waking life. How well you cope with the storm is an indicator of your confidence related to your ability to cope. Are you seeking shelter from the storm or are your closing the storm windows and gathering emergency supplies? While storms indicate a difficult period, the good news is that a storm brings calm, and that is always welcome after a period of hardship.

Strangling

Strangling suggests an inability to communicate emotions due to external force. This dream is one of aggression, and your subconscious is acknowledging the violence and potential danger of suppressing your emotions.

Suffocating

Dreaming of being suffocated is an indication that you are not fully expressing your emotional or sexual desires. Are you afraid of criticism? Conflict? Consider who or what may not be allowing you to breathe, then face that person or problem head-on.

Suicide

If you are angry with yourself for something you did or said, it may manifest in a dream about your own suicide. Don't take this dream too seriously. Subconsciously, you are acknowledging a desire to let go of the aspect of yourself that you do not like and that has caused you to act out of character.

Summer

Summer represents the mature or adult phase of your life. If you dream of an activity taking place during the summer months, the dream is emphasizing that particular period. Your feelings in the dream indicate your attitude toward this particular phase of life. For example, if you have an anxiety-provoking dream that takes place during the summer, you may be afraid to grow up.

Sun

The sun represents awareness or your spiritual nature. A sunrise suggests the onset of awareness and a sunset suggests the completion of your spiritual journey. Consider the phase of spiritual awareness you are in to provide further meaning to your dream.

Swimming

Dreaming about swimming means you are exploring your conscious life experiences and emotions. When you swim, you are often unaware of what is below the surface, particularly in the ocean, so swimming involves a leap of faith in your ability to navigate in unknown waters. If you are having difficulty swimming or are drowning, you are experiencing difficulty in your waking life and feel overwhelmed by your emotions. Are you swimming against the tide? This indicates that you are facing opposition or challenges from others. Swimming dreams confirm that despite potentially unknown and unforeseen challenges you are confident in facing you life experiences and emotions. This would be a good time to deal with a situation you may have been avoiding because you feared rejection or embarrassment.

Table

Tables are the foundation of many family and community rituals, such as mealtimes, conversations, and negotiations. The function of the table provides further clues about the dream's meaning. For example, a classroom table suggests collaboration in learning; a dining room table indicates family dynamics. Note your position at the table, as well as its condition. Consider your current relationships and ask yourself how well you are connecting with others. A social or professional meeting may be in order to resolve a current conflict.

Talking

Most dreams involve conversation, as speech is our primary method to communicate with others. Often, your ability to communicate in your dreams is different from your daily life. For example, if you are normally talkative and find yourself withdrawn and quiet in your dreams, your subconscious may be suggesting that you need to spend more time listening to others. If you have difficulty speaking in your dreams, you may feel misunderstood in your waking life.

Tattoo

A tattoo symbolizes a memory or experience that has made a permanent impression on you. Seemingly inconsequential events that took place in your waking life may appear in your dreams because they have left a permanent impression in your subconscious. If possible, determine the image that is tattooed on you as it may point to the memory that needs be resurrected and examined in your waking life.

Taxi

If you dream about a taxi, then you desire assistance in navigating your life's course. You feel that you cannot take control of your own life's path and have exhausted all other options that may have led to recklessness. You can't always be in control. You should hire a life coach and take yourself out of the driver's seat in order to gain some perspective regarding where your life is headed.

Teacher

Dreaming of a teacher indicates your desire for knowledge and guidance. Are you in need of a spiritual guide or mentor who may help you see things in a new perspective? Do not be ashamed to seek out the help of others when needed.

Telephone

Telephones are unique methods of communication in that they do not allow people to communicate face to face. Telephones allow you to talk with someone that you might not be able to speak with in person due to physical or emotional limitations. They also allow you to avoid speaking with someone, because you do not have to answer the telephone if you do not feel like communicating with anyone. Effective communication can only take place face-to-face, and dreaming of the telephone suggests avoidance. Stop screening your calls and schedule some face time with key individuals in your life.

Television

Watching television in your dreams suggests that you are passively obtaining information in you waking life. Pay careful attention to what you are watching in your dream, as the characters are likely aspects of yourself that your subconscious is asking you to recognize.

Tent

Tents provide inexpensive housing for people on the move. Do you feel a sense of impermanence in your waking life? Dreaming about a tent implies that you have anxiety about establishing permanent roots.

Throat

The throat represents communication and the fear of self-expression. Despite your feelings of vulnerability, communication must be necessary, otherwise your subconscious mind wouldn't have bothered bringing this image to your dream world.

Thunder

Thunder represents the disruptive and disturbing thoughts that hover near the surface of your consciousness and cause feelings of restlessness. Dreaming about thunder is a warning for you to examine your distracting thoughts and attempt to quiet them.

Tickling

Dreaming of tickling suggests a desire to release emotions that you normally confine. Perhaps you hope that your new boyfriend will make the first move toward sexual intimacy since you are normally shy and reserved, or you may feel the need to engage in a fun childlike activity, such as biking or playing outdoors. This dream is a reminder to lighten up and have fun.

Tiger

A tiger represents your sexual habits and urges, particularly as they relate to your feelings of control or power. Are you in a sexual relationship where you have acquired power or power has shifted? If a tiger is attacking you, ask yourself if you feel that you have lost the upper hand in your waking life. If you are trying to hunt or capture the tiger, ask yourself why you are trying to control your sexual urges.

Toilet

Are you containing emotions that need to be privately released? If so, you may dream of a toilet. A toilet represents those emotions that you deem unnecessary or embarrassing and that you hope to eliminate. A clogged toilet represents repressed emotions, and cleaning a toilet suggests that you are no longer embarrassed about your emotions.

Tool

Your feelings about your ability to handle practical matters are symbolized through tools that appear in your dreams. Tools are positive dream symbols that relate to your ability to repair and rebuild relationships with resources you have at hand. For example, dreaming of a drill represents an issue that needs to be examined further, and a saw indicates a relationship that needs to be severed in order to further your personal development.

Tooth

Teeth represent the ability to digest knowledge. Information is available in many forms and your ability to seek out and absorb knowledge can lead to personal growth. Dreaming about losing your teeth means that you feel that you are losing control in your waking life. Consider what aspect of your life is beginning to get the best of you, then seek out the information and tools you need to make smart choices.

Tower

Towers, like other buildings, represent the self, and your position in the tower suggests your position in life relative to others. If you are in the tower, you are likely feeling confident, or even boastful, in your waking life. Dreaming of another person in a tower brings back memories of the damsel in distress and indicates that there is someone in your life who needs to be rescued. This dream may be an indication that your feelings of superiority may cause future loneliness and isolation.

Toy

Dreaming about toys indicates the need to return to childlike pleasures and pursuits. You may be taking life too seriously or examining a problem from a strictly rational point of view. Imagination and creativity are the hallmarks of childhood toys and games, and applying these attributes to your waking life may help you solve a complex or frustrating situation.

Train

A train represents our life's journey within our community of family, friends, and peers. Unlike other methods of transportation, trains have a predetermined destination. Where do you feel that your life is headed?

Transportation

All methods of transportation represent our life's journey and provide clues as to how you are navigating your life's path. See separate listings for bicycle, boat, bus, car, driving, motorcycle, plane, railway, and train.

Trap

Dreaming of being trapped in a situation or environment suggests feelings of isolation and confinement in your waking life. Escape indicates that you are ready to let go of outdated or negative attitudes.

Treasure

Treasure hunting often involves history, an old map, a long journey, and numerous obstacles. Dreaming about a treasure obviously represents something of value, but also the planning and hard work associated with its attainment. If you have recently made a step forward in an important relationship, you may dream about treasure hunting. This is an indication that although you are still searching for ways to achieve intimacy and understanding, you value the relationship and feel confident that your hard work will pay off.

Tree

A tree represents the physical, emotional, and spiritual aspects of self as a powerful and unified whole. The roots represent your physical connection to the earth through your body, family, and cultural roots; the trunk represents your energy and growth; and the branches represent the varied aspects of your life. Examine the condition of the tree. New buds may indicate a beginning or fertility, falling leaves represent aspects of our life that are fading or falling.

Trophy

A trophy is a symbol of outstanding achievement and dreaming about receiving a trophy is a congratulatory dream. If recognition is withheld from you in your dream, then you are feeling unappreciated in your waking life.

Trumpet

Whether heralding the arrival of royalty or playing a solo rendition of "Taps," trumpets indicate an announcement. When a trumpet appears in your dreams, pay careful attention to what follows, as this is the main point of your dream.

Trunk

A trunk represents old memories or attitudes. If you are rummaging through a trunk, then you are interested in exploring your past. A locked trunk indicates that your past is inaccessible to you. While it is useful to understand your past, you must live in the present. Do not obsess about your past experiences.

Tunnel

A tunnel represents a period of transition from one stage of life to the next, usually a stage marked by exploration of the subconscious. Because there is only one way in and out of a tunnel, it can also symbolize dark and frightening aspects of the subconscious. If there is a light at the end of the tunnel, then you believe that you are coming to the end of this phase in your life.

Turtle

When removed from their shells, turtles are soft and defenseless creatures. Their shells offer protection and allow them to withdraw when necessary. Sound like someone you know? You may dream about turtles during a period in your life when you feel you need protection. Practicing patience and steadfastness, two important attributes of the turtle, is the best course of action.

Twins

Twins represent the dual nature of your personality. There exists in every person the propensity toward good and evil and kindness and cruelty. If the twins are generally amiable, this suggests that the two sides of your personality are in harmony. If, on the other hand, the twins are fighting, pay careful attention to which twin wins the brawl. This is the side of your personality that is taking over and needs to be more carefully controlled.

UFO

If you dream of a UFO, your subconscious is acknowledging an aspect of yourself or an experience that is unfamiliar. Do you feel alien in your own body? Has a recent experience shaken your belief system and made you feel that your life more closely resembles a scene from *Close Encounters of the Third Kind*? When UFO dreams involve interaction with aliens, this is an indication that you need to spend time exploring your deepest and darkest attitudes and emotions.

Umbrella

When you are going through a difficult period in your life, you may dream about an umbrella. This is a reminder from your subconscious that you have resources that may offer you security and protection. This may be either physical or emotional security depending on your situation. Seek assistance to successfully survive this period.

Underground

Subconscious experiences or emotions are often revealed in underground dream scenes, such as caves, tunnels, or subterranean urban centers. Dreams provide you with opportunities to better understand your subconscious desires, and dreams that take place underground often provide you with the most obvious messages.

Undress

Because clothes represent the way we appear to the outside world, undressing indicates your desire to be stripped of all pretenses. Dreaming of being in your underwear suggests a desire to reveal your sexuality. Perhaps you have not been authentic in your professional or personal life and now you want people to see you for who you really are. This dream indicates that you are no longer afraid of being vulnerable.

Unemployment

Fear of failure may drive dreams of unemployment. Have you recently experienced a setback at work? Do you feel that your talents are not being noticed?

Unicorn

These mystical creatures represent your childhood and the innocence and imagination that accompany it. Unicorns are positive dream symbols that suggest harmony with these aspects of your personality. This would be an excellent time to begin a new creative project if you haven't already.

Uniform

If you are wearing the uniform, consider the role attached to that particular uniform. For example, a nurse's uniform suggests nurturing, whereas a police officer's uniform represents authority. Dreaming of wearing a particular uniform means that you identify with that group.

Urine

Urinating signifies the release of repressed sexual emotions. Your ability to control this bodily function is an indication of your ability to control your sexual desires.

Vacation

Your life's journey may be difficult right now and your subconscious is encouraging you to relax. Schedule some time away.

Vagina

Dreaming about the vagina is an indication to embrace your feminine attributes. This is true for men and women. The vagina represents nurturing, fertility, receptiveness, creativity, and intuition.

Vampire

Relationships that are destructive or draining are often revealed in dreams about vampires. If you dream of a vampire, consider who or what is robbing you of energy. If you are the vampire in the dream, then your dream is an indication that you are depending on others for your happiness.

Vase

A vase represents the beauty and growth inherent in your relationships. Dreaming about a vase suggests that you are receptive to new experiences and relationships. An empty vase suggests a lack of growth in your relationships.

Vegetable

Dreaming about vegetables suggests that you have physical needs that are not being met in your waking life. Because the earth represents stability and solidity, dreaming about harvesting vegetables, particularly root vegetables, indicates your desire to find stability in your waking life.

Victim

While many dreams are violent, repeatedly dreaming about being victimized is an indication that you feel you have no control over the events in your life. Your subconscious will continue to replay these nightmares until you begin to receive their messages. Specifically, that you are responsible for your actions and must take ownership of both the good and bad things that happen in your life.

Violence

Violent dreams are caused by destructive or negative thoughts in your waking life. You may be experiencing internal conflict and this is expressed in your dreams. The only way to end unpleasant violent dreams is to deal with your negative thoughts and emotions in your waking life.

Virgin

Dreams about virginity relate more to a purity of mind than to purity of body. Your soul is your most authentic self, and dreams about virginity are indications that you are connecting to your soul.

Volcano

An inactive volcano represents potentially destructive repressed emotions. This may not be the best time to confront someone about a past trauma. An erupting volcano indicates that your emotions have become out of control and that the resulting explosion may lead to self destruction.

Wading

Water represents your conscious life experiences, particularly emotions, and wading through water indicates that you are slowly immersing yourself in your emotions. The flow of the water, its depth, and your ability to wade through it provide further information about the depth of your exploration and the difficulty or ease you are experiencing. If you dream about wading through water, it is a good indication to continue on your journey of self-exploration.

Waiting

When you spend a night of dreams seated in the doctor's office or standing in line at the checkout counter, your subconscious is attempting to teach you a lesson about patience. Depending on your current situation, the dream may be an indication to practice patience and stop rushing toward an end result. Or, the dream may be a sign to stop waiting for other people or circumstances to propel your life forward.

Walking

Your outlook regarding your progress in life is represented in how you walk through your dream world. The meaning applied to postures and body language in waking life is applicable to your dream. For example, dragging your feet with your head lowered suggests defeat, while a head held high suggests confidence and purpose. Also, consider the direction you are headed. Are you walking aimlessly or with purpose?

Wallet

Your wallet contains valuable personal information and resources, particularly your identification and money. Losing your wallet is a common dream theme and suggests that you are fearful of losing your identity and financial resources. Hire a financial planner, open a 401K, and put your money worries to bed.

Wall

Walls symbolize barriers in thinking. Do you carry a belief that limits you? Have you constructed a wall between you and someone you care about?

War

Intense internal conflict will manifest in your dreams as war. Unlike natural disasters, war is planned conflict and as such suggests that the conflict you are experiencing was predetermined by your own actions. If you cannot resolve your conflict through negotiations, it may be time to hang the white flag over your door.

Warehouse

A dream that takes place in a warehouse is a reflection about a memory or piece of your past that you have temporarily set aside.

Washing

Washing signifies ridding yourself of negative attitudes or beliefs related to a particular part of your life. Washing clothes suggests a desire to clean up your outward appearance, washing your hands indicates your desire to disassociate yourself with something you have done, and washing the dishes may represent a desire to streamline your domestic life.

Watching

Are you a voyeur in your dreams? Consider what you are observing in your dream. The subconscious picks up more information in a day than we can consciously recognize. Your subconscious may be trying to point out something you have overlooked. If you are more generally observing the actions and activities of others, this may be an indication that you are not actively participating in your own life.

Water

Water represents your conscious day-to-day experiences, particularly emotions. Water symbols are powerful and plentiful. You may travel on water via boat, you may swim or bathe in it, or drink it. The possibilities are endless. The clarity, depth, and movement of the water will determine your attitude toward your conscious experiences. As is true of any other object in your dreams, how you relate to water is just as meaningful as its symbolic meaning. See separate listings for bath, diving, drowning, dam, flood, fountain, island, ocean, waterfall, and waves.

Waterfall

Powerful, free flowing emotions that often overwhelm your everyday life experiences are represented by waterfalls. If you are standing under a waterfall, then you feel overwhelmed by your emotions.

Wave

Waves represent the ups and downs of everyday life. Your ability to ride the waves in your dreams is an indication of your ability to cope. Are the waves gentle and lulling or have you found yourself caught in a tsunami?

Weather

Our moods and emotions are often represented by the weather conditions in our dreams. To interpret weather, consider the metaphorical moods in waking life. For example, one is said to have a sunny disposition or to have a black cloud hanging over his head. The sun equates to feelings of happiness, clouds signify depression, and rain a release of emotions. Of course, we cannot control the weather. Understand that this dream is an indication to accept that you cannot control external influences and should work with what you are given.

Wedding

A wedding represents the desire to unify two different yet complementary aspects of your personality into a cohesive whole. Consider the qualities of the person you are marrying in your dream and ask yourself if this is a quality you are striving to attain.

Whale

Whales represent enormous, and often overwhelming, emotions that you fear may engulf you. Whatever situation you are facing in your waking life, it is one that has tremendous emotional power over you. You may need to consult a trusted friend or advisor to find strength.

Wheel

Car or bicycle wheels, water wheels, and Ferris wheels are symbolic of the cyclical nature of your life. Like most cyclical objects, wheels are reminders of the universal nature of the human experience. If you feel out of synch with the natural rhythms of life or that you are no longer moving forward, it may be represented in your dream as a missing wheel or a malfunctioning Ferris wheel.

Whistle

Whistles typically appear in dreams to grab your attention. A blowing whistle may signify the completion of a particular phase of your life, or may serve as a warning, so pay careful attention to the events following the whistle in your dream. If you or someone else is absentmindedly whistling in the dream, this indicates contentment in your waking life.

White

When white is a predominant color in your dream, it indicates purity and wholeness. If you or the subject in your dream is bathed in white light, then you are acknowledging your spiritual enlightenment and your subconscious is reminding you of your ability to protect and defend yourself against harm.

Wig

A wig or toupee represents false attitudes or beliefs. For example, have you recently adopted new political or religious opinions to fit in with a particular social group? Taking steps toward self-awareness will help you uncover your core values and beliefs and will allow you to drop the façade.

Wind

Wind represents your thoughts, and the wind's movement in your dream indicates the changes that you are experiencing in life. If you notice that the wind picks up suddenly, you may be going through an unexpected change in thinking caused by external sources. If the wind is violent and gusty, you may be experiencing rapid change that is leaving behind remnants of destruction.

Window

How you view life is highlighted in your dreams by viewing the world, situations, and people through windows. An open window suggests a desire to connect with whatever is on the other side, whereas a closed or jammed window suggests an inability to connect. If you are watching a person through the window, consider whether the object of your attention notices you. The person's acknowledgment or lack thereof is a good indication of your desire to make your feelings or opinions about the person known.

Winter

The cycle of life is represented by the seasons, and winter represents the final phase of the life cycle. If you believe in reincarnation, winter may also carry the positive connotation of preparation for rebirth. You may fear aging, and this fear may appear as winter in your dreams. Or, you may be going through a period of inactivity in your life. Take comfort in the knowledge that a change and growth are around the corner.

Witch

The female witch symbol provides insight regarding your creativity, superstition, and intuition. If the dream was generally pleasant, you should assume that you are comfortable with and rely regularly upon these qualities within yourself. If, on the other hand, the dream caused anxiety, you may fear aspects of yourself that are not grounded in reason.

Witness

To dream of a witness suggests being called upon to examine an aspect of your life publicly and honestly. Have you been keeping a secret against your better judgment that could affect the well-being of others? Are you hiding your true intentions? When you see yourself as a witness in your dream, you need to pay careful attention to the situation you are witnessing in your waking life.

Wolf

Wolves are known for their prowess and cunning natures and dreaming about wolves highlights these instincts. You may be showing signs of aggression, anger, or deception in your waking life, and you fear the outcome of your actions. If the dream is not fear provoking, the wolf may appear as a guide in your dream and may lead you to answers about your life's purpose if you follow it.

Womb

The womb represents creativity, fertility, and security. If you are feeling overwhelmed, you may dream of the womb in a compensatory attempt to withdraw from life. The prenatal state is representative of innocence and purity and the dream is an indication to reconnect with this state in order to achieve further development.

Wood

Your long-held beliefs based on tradition and past experience are represented through wood in your dreams. The wood may appear as furniture, toys, or trees. Your relationship to the object is integral to understanding the symbolism of your dream. For example, cutting down wood suggests disassociating from your belief system, and rotting wood reveals that something or someone has corrupted your thinking. Being lost in the woods is a common dream theme and depicts your confusion and lack of direction.

Writing

Writing reveals your desire for self-expression and creativity. If the content of the writing is clear, this is a form of communication from your subconscious self to your conscious self.

X,Y,Z

X ray

X rays represent introspection. In general, dreams about X rays are dreams about your desire to gain insight into your subconscious desires and emotions. The part of the body being x-rayed may provide further information. For example, an X ray of the head indicates a desire to examine your beliefs.

Yellow

The appearance of the color yellow magnifies the hope, happiness, and energy in your dream.

Youth

Youth appears in dreams to remind you of the qualities you exemplified at that age. It is likely that you are currently experiencing many of the same fears or hopes that you did in your youth. The key to utilizing this dream symbol is to analyze how you coped with these issues during that time and learn from your past mistakes and/or successes.

Zebra

The zebra represents the qualities of the horse, such as strength, stamina, and speed, but further emphasizes your ability to reject these attributes. In order to incorporate these positive attributes into your life, you will need to balance your waking life.

Zipper

Zipping something in your dream suggests a desire for connection and unity in your life, whereas unzipping suggests a desire to break away from an attitude or belief that is no longer useful or necessary. A stuck or broken zipper is an indication that you feel caught between independence and your desire to connect with others.

Zodiac

As you begin to interpret your dreams and embark on the path to self-discovery, you may dream of the zodiac, most likely your own sun sign. Seeing your zodiac symbol is a reminder of your basic traits and characteristics. Dreaming of many zodiac symbols or the zodiac as a whole is an indication that you are beginning to connect your life to the collective conscious of the universe.

Zoo

Your caged instincts and desires are revealed in dreams that take place in a zoo. If you notice a particular animal in your dream, look up its meaning and consider whether you are repressing those qualities.

BIBLIOGRAPHY

Books

Ball, Pamela. *The Complete Dream Dictionary*. Edison: Chartwell Books, 2000.

Condron, Barbara. *The Dreamer's Dictionary: Translations in the Universal Language of Mind*. Windyville: School of Metaphysics, 1994.

Crisp, Tony. *Dream Dictionary: An A to Z Guide to Understanding Your Unconscious Mind*. New York: Dell Publishing, 1990.

Cummings, Carol. *The Sex of Your Dreams: Erotic Dreams and Their Hidden Meanings*. Gloucester: Fair Winds Press, 2003.

Web Sites

www.dreamjournal.org

www.soulfuture.com

www.spiritcommunity.com

ABOUT THE AUTHOR

Candice Janco is a freelance writer whose work has appeared in bridal magazines, tourist publications, and newspapers. She lives with her husband and chocolate Labrador retriever in Charlotte, North Carolina.